The CMIO Survival Guide

A Handbook for Chief Medical Information Officers
and Those Who Hire Them

Second Edition

T0272097

The CMIO Survival Guide

A Handbook for Chief Medical Information Officers
and Those Who Hire Them

Second Edition

Richard L. Rydell, MBA, LFHIMSS, FACHE, Editor

Howard M. Landa, MD, Associate Editor

CRC Press
Taylor & Francis Group
Boca Raton   London   New York

CRC Press is an imprint of the
Taylor & Francis Group, an **informa** business

A PRODUCTIVITY PRESS BOOK

CRC Press
Taylor & Francis Group
6000 Broken Sound Parkway NW, Suite 300
Boca Raton, FL 33487-2742

**Visit the Taylor & Francis Web site at
http://www.taylorandfrancis.com**

**and the CRC Press Web site at
http://www.crcpress.com**

Contents

Introduction

The Chief Medical Information Officer (CMIO or CHIO or whatever new moniker comes into fashion) must have a deep understanding of both the workflows and the science that underlies the delivery of healthcare. This, aligned with our requisite knowledge of healthcare information technology is the key to the value we provide to our healthcare organizations.

This book is intended to be a pocket handbook for the new CMIO. It will be a valued "quick guide" organized by topics that the CMIO deals with on a regular basis. The key to the value of this handbook is the accumulated experience and lessons learned of the Association of Medical Directors of Information Systems (AMDIS) faculty that contributed to its content. This book is also a concise guide to picking the right CMIO job and helping him or her be successful.

It may never be known when the electronic medical record physician-champion graduated to adopting the title of CMIO, or where we will go next. We have lived through the years when discussions about first generation electronic medical records yielded quizzical at best, or at worst, contemptuous looks from colleagues. We are now in the era of the nearly ubiquitous Electronic Health Record (or perhaps moving towards "Comprehensive Health Records?") and if anything, looks are even more polarized than quizzical/contemptuous. The phenomenon of physician burnout is multifactorial but the EHR has become its lightning rod. Most will admit that an EHR is truly required to access the information necessary to provide the best care, but we all acknowledge that the systems have not kept up with increasingly complicated patients who expect more and more from modern technology. We are on the crest of a wave that will leverage AI (artificial intelligence) and machine learning; advanced imaging; and enhanced analytics to finally deliver on the promise of improving quality, efficiency, and both patient and clinician satisfaction. It is these tools that will be available to the progressively greater number of young men and women we see extending their training in medicine to preparation for leadership in medical informatics. And it is to them that this book is dedicated; and to those who would seek to understand why they have made this career choice, to those who hire them in these roles, and hopefully to assist them in this transformation of healthcare.

The structure of this book is brief, targeted, and to the point, in keeping with the new literary style that has appeared in the last decades with the advent of the World Wide Web. It is our intention to periodically update and revise the contents of this manual, in keeping with the rapidly changing field of medical informatics, and the roles of the CMIO.

The authors of this book represent many of the leaders of AMDIS, but we would be remiss if we did not recognize the wisdom that is provided by all the members of our esteemed organization that provided for the core knowledge that we share with you today.

Richard L. Rydell, MBA, LFHIMSS, FACHE
Howard M. Landa, MD
William F. Bria, MD, FCCP, FHIMSS

Editors

Richard L. Rydell, MBA, LFHIMSS, FACHE, is a founder and CEO of the Association of Medical Directors of Information Systems (AMDIS), the premier physician membership organization dedicated to advancing the field of applied medical informatics. Mr. Rydell has a distinguished career as a healthcare executive, serving as a senior vice president and chief information officer at Memorial Health Services, Long Beach; Stanford University Medical Center; and Baystate Health Services. He is a fellow in the American College of Healthcare Executives and a fellow and life member of the Healthcare Information and Management Systems Society (HIMSS). He served as national president of HIMSS and was a founding board member and vice chairman of the College of Healthcare Information Management Executives (CHIME). Mr. Rydell is the coauthor of the popular books, *The Physician-Computer Connection and The Physician-Computer Conundrum* (Taylor and Francis, 2004) and coeditor of the first edition of *The CMIO Survival Guide* (Jossey-Bass, 1996). Mr. Rydell serves as an elected board member of the Seneca Healthcare District, Chester, California. He was recognized as one of the "HIMSS 50 in 50," a recognition of 50 individuals who contributed significantly to the field of healthcare information technology and the improvement of healthcare through technology, in the 50 years since HIMSS was founded.

Howard M. Landa, MD, did two years of surgical residency 1983–85 at NYU and Bellevue. He trained in urology at the University of California-San Diego and completed a fellowship in pediatric urology at Texas Children's Hospital, Houston, Texas.

After training, Dr. Landa joined the Loma Linda University, Loma Linda, California to practice pediatric urology and during his first year he built a document management system to help the practice manage transcribed documents and he became the director of Medical Informatics for Loma Linda University Medical Center in 1996. He joined Kaiser Hawaii in 2001 to practice pediatric urology and act as one of their physician IT champions, and became their chief medical information officer (CMIO) in 2005. He was the physician lead for both Kaiser's national downtime project and the operating room software; and under his leadership Kaiser Hawaii completed the EHR implementation, attaining HIMSS level 6 two months after inpatient go-live and Level 7 in 2012. From 2009–2017 he was the CMIO of the Alameda Health System and led multiple EHR implementations and optimizations.

In 2017, he joined Sutter Health as their vice president of Clinical Informatics and EHR. He has been the program director and vice-chair of the Association of Medical Directors of Information Systems (AMDIS) since 1997; the chair of the HIMSS/AMDIS Physician Community 2011–2013; and was named one of the top 25 clinical informaticists in 2010–12.

Contributors

Raymond Aller. Dr. Aller has devoted his career to advancing and teaching clinical informatics. His MD thesis at Harvard Medical School entailed design and deployment of the first online surgical pathology information system, which has served as the prototype for most of today's commercially available systems. He has guided hospitals in the implementation of diverse healthcare information systems, in several cases functioning as CMIO long before the word had been invented. He helped to develop the first edition of SNOMED, the concepts of HL7, and later, the LOINC system for exchanging laboratory and pathology results. For over 30 years, he has edited Newsbytes, one of the most widely read columns on healthcare informatics. In 1991, he launched the proposal to create an ABMS-endorsed board certification in clinical informatics – this reached fruition with the first certification examination in 2013. He has championed many other forward-looking initiatives in clinical informatics, including the early-1990's campaign to identify all blood specimens with a barcoded wristband, and more recently, the use of positive biometric identifiers in every healthcare venue. Most recently, he has focused his attention on strengthening laboratory information systems in low-income countries.

Pam Arlotto, President & CEO, Maestro Strategies. Pam Arlotto works with CEOs, Boards and the C-Suite to develop strategies for high-value healthcare. She is President and

CEO of Maestro Strategies an Atlanta-based healthcare management consulting firm. She is a former National Chair of the Healthcare Information & Management Systems Society (HIMSS). She has worked with AMDIS to develop the CMIO Crash Course: A Survival Guide and wrote the white paper "From the Playing Field to the Press Box: The Emerging Role of the Chief Health Information Officer. She is well known for the award-winning book series, Beyond Return on Investment: Expanding the Value of Healthcare Information Technology. She was the founding Chair of the Center for Healthcare Information Management and has served on the Boards of The Georgia Tech Foundation, The Wallace H. Coulter Department of Biomedical Engineering at the Georgia Institute of Technology & Emory University School of Medicine, the Scheller School of Business, and the Georgia Tech Alumni Association. She currently serves on advisory boards for several privately held healthcare companies.

Sameer Badlani, MD, FACP, is the Chief Health Information Officer & System Vice-President for Sutter Health. His areas of accountability include clinical informatics, digital health, enterprise analytics and data management. His areas of interest include the potential use of behavioral psychology in the delivery of health care, engaging clinical providers and translating the value of analytics and informatics in the clinical and business domains. As an advisor to startups in various stages, he supports their journey to value creation and product delivery, while engaging with VCs on portfolio and investment thesis.

Dr. Badlani speaks nationally, educates and consults on topics in digital medicine, clinical informatics, analytics, and innovation. In 2013, he was recognized in Crain's Chicago 2013: 40 under 40 and nominated to the board of AMDIS, the premier international organization of CMIOs and executive physician leaders in Informatics. Recently, he was nominated to the Becker's 2017 list of top 50 Health System CMIOs.

He received his medical degree from the University of Delhi in India. After completing his internal medicine residency training, Dr. Badlani served as chief resident at the University of Oklahoma in Tulsa. He also received training in bio-medical informatics at the University of Utah in Salt Lake City. At the University of Chicago, his clinical practice was focused on solid organ transplant and oncology in the inpatient setting.

Previous roles include faculty and CMIO at the University of Chicago Medicine and Biological Sciences followed by CHIO for Intermountain Healthcare.

Albert S. Chan, MD, MS, serves as Chief of Digital Patient Experience at Sutter Health, leading the digital transformation of one of the largest integrated health systems in the United States. In this interdisciplinary role, Dr. Chan leads an omni-channel patient engagement strategy that spans patient outreach via the patient portal My Health Online, telemedicine, and tech-forward customer support via online chat and artificial intelligence-powered solutions. He is also the executive pacesetter for patient access, leading Sutter's modernization of its scheduling practices and navigation of healthcare services. In addition, Dr. Chan provides leadership for the development and scaling of innovative partnerships, spearheading translation of innovation into his own clinical practice and those of his colleagues.

Dedicated to physician and patient empowerment through health information technology in his current role and previously as CMIO of the Palo Alto Medical Foundation, Albert was awarded the fourth Epic PAC Academy Award (2014) by his peers for contributions to the Epic Systems Corporation community. In 2017, Dr. Chan was named to the Fulbright Specialist Roster and awarded an Eisenhower Fellowship.

Dr. Chan earned a B.S. in Biological Sciences from Stanford University and M.D. from the University of California, San Diego. After completing residency and chief residency in family medicine, Albert concurrently completed fellowships in Biomedical Informatics at Stanford University School of Medicine and family medicine research at the University of California, San Francisco School of Medicine. During fellowship, he joined the team that launched PAMFOnline, one of the first linked personal health records in the United States.

Richard Gibson, MD, PhD, is the Executive Director of the Health Record Banking Alliance (http://www.healthbanking.org/), a non-profit organization founded in 2006 to promote consumer-centered, consumer-controlled, comprehensive, lifetime health records. Dr. Gibson comes to HRBA from Gartner, Inc., where he was a Research Director. Previously, he held roles as Chief of Healthcare Intelligence at Providence Health & Services, Chief Information Officer at Legacy Health in Portland, and Chief Medical Information Officer at Providence Health System, Oregon Region. He is an Affiliate Assistant Professor in the Department of Medical Informatics and Clinical Epidemiology at Oregon Health and Science University. Dr. Gibson's educational background includes a BS from Stanford University, an MD from Case Western Reserve University, a PhD in Medical Informatics from the University of Utah with a fellowship at Intermountain Health Care in Salt Lake City, and an MBA from the Wharton School. Dr. Gibson is a retired family physician and emergency physician.

William Hersh, MD, FACMI, FACP, is professor and chair of the Department of Medical Informatics and Clinical Epidemiology in the School of Medicine at Oregon Health and Science University (OHSU) in Portland, Oregon. Dr. Hersh is a leader and innovator in biomedical informatics both in education and research. He serves as director of the OHSU Biomedical Informatics Graduate Program, which includes two masters degrees (research and professional), a PhD degree, and graduate certificate. Dr. Hersh has won numerous awards for his innovations. These include the OHSU Faculty Senate

Distinguished Faculty Award for outstanding teaching in 2007;
the 2008 AMIA Donald A.B. Lindberg Award for Innovation
in Informatics; one of the Modern Healthcare Top 25 Clinical
Informaticists in 2010, 2011, and 2012; and the HIMSS
Physician Leadership Award in 2015. He is an elected fellow of
the American College of Medical Informatics and the American
College of Physicians. Dr. Hersh also maintains a web site
(http://www.billhersh.info) and the Informatics Professor blog
(http://informaticsprofessor.blogspot.com/).

Dr. Eric M. Liederman, MD, serves as director of Medical
Informatics for The Permanente Medical Group and National
Leader of Privacy, Security and IT Infrastructure for The
Permanente Federation, of Kaiser Permanente, which serves
over 12 million members across the United States. In these
roles, Dr. Liederman is accountable for privacy and security, IT
investment, large program governance, and IT infrastructure
delivery and resilience.

Prior to joining TPMG in 2005, Dr. Liederman served
as medical director of Clinical Information Systems for the
University of California Davis Health System, where he led the
successful transition from paper medical records to a vendor
electronic health record (EHR) and patient portal. Earlier, Dr.
Liederman served as medical director of Information Systems
for Mercy Healthcare Sacramento and MedClinic Medical Group.

Dr. Liederman served as a Lieutenant Commander in the
U.S. Navy, where, as squadron flight surgeon, he ensured the
medical readiness of a Marine Corps Expeditionary Force with
which he deployed to the Persian Gulf for Operation Desert
Storm.

Dr. Liederman has published, and speaks internationally
on topics including knowledge management, patient
e-connectivity, collaboration with IT, and privacy and security.
He earned his Bachelor's degree from Dartmouth College, his
MD from Tufts University, and his MPH from the University of
Massachusetts, Amherst.

Christopher Longhurst. As Chief Information Officer of UC San Diego Health, Dr. Longhurst is responsible for all operations and strategic planning for information and communications technology across the multiple hospitals, clinics, and professional schools. Dr. Longhurst is also a Clinical Professor of Biomedical Informatics and Pediatrics at UC San Diego School of Medicine, and continues to see patients. He previously served as Chief Medical Information Officer for Stanford Children's Health and Clinical Professor at the Stanford University School of Medicine, where he helped to lead the organization through the implementation of a comprehensive electronic medical record (EMR) for over a decade. This work culminated in HIMSS stage 7 awards for both Lucile Packard Children's Hospital and 167 network practices in Stanford Children's Health.

Dr. Longhurst has published dozens of scientific articles in peer-reviewed journals on how technology and data can improve patient care and outcomes and was elected as a fellow in the prestigious American College of Medical Informatics, among other distinctions. He is a board-certified pediatrician and clinical informaticist, and founded Stanford's fellowship in clinical informatics, first in the nation to receive accreditation. Described as a pragmatic academician, Dr. Longhurst serves as an advisor to several companies and speaks internationally on a wide gamut of healthcare IT topics.

Ronald W. Louks, MD, MBA, is the Medical Director of CPSI (a publicly traded company), a leading provider of healthcare IT solutions and services for community hospitals and post-acute care facilities. CPSI offers acute care EHR solutions from its Evident and Healthland companies, and a post-acute care EHR solution from American HealthTech.

With his background as a practicing Internal Medicine specialist and Healthcare Administrator for 27 years prior to joining CPSI in 2012, Dr. Louks is frequently sought out by executive and physician leaders to help develop and advocate

strategies for physician EHR adoption and optimization
that include improving proficiency, reduction of error rates,
increasing accuracy of clinical documentation, and enhancing
patient safety measures. He also works internally with the CPSI
family of companies to develop and improve policies related
to patient care products, and provides physician leadership for
EHR product development, implementation, and adoption.

Dr. Louks was awarded the degree of Bachelor of Science
from the College of Science at Purdue University in West
Lafayette, IN, where he was inducted into Phi Beta Kappa,
Zeta chapter, as an undergraduate. After earning his MD from
Indiana University School of Medicine in Indianapolis, IN, he
completed a residency in Internal Medicine at Ball Memorial
Hospital in Muncie, IN, followed by an additional year there
as Chief Resident of Internal Medicine. He later received
an MBA from Ball State University in Muncie, IN, where he
was inducted into the honorary management society, Sigma
Iota Epsilon. Dr. Louks maintains active membership in the
Phi Beta Kappa Society and is a lifetime member of the
President's Council of Purdue University. He is also a member of
the American College of Physicians (ACP), the Association
of Medical Directors of Information Systems (AMDIS) and in
2005 was named a Vanguard member of the American College
of Physician Executives (ACPE). He has practiced and held
several administrative positions in Indiana and Idaho, including
successful entrepreneurial ventures as well as employed
positions with both small and large healthcare systems.

Dr. Michael J. McCoy, MD, has diverse experiences as a
practicing clinician, a physician executive in the electronic
health record vendor community, a national consultant, and as
the first chief health information officer for The Office of the
National Coordinator for Health Information Technology (ONC).

He previously served as the first chief medical information
officer for a large faith-based Integrated Delivery Network (IDN).
Trained as an OB/GYN, he was chief of the OB/GYN department

for Noble Army Hospital post residency. He had a collaborative solo private practice of obstetrics and gynecology for more than 20 years, and was an early adopter of EMR systems.

He served as The American College/Congress of Obstetricians and Gynecologists' national health information technology strategist, participating in Certification Commission for Healthcare Information Technology (CCHIT), Integrating the Healthcare Enterprise (IHE), Healthcare Information Technology Standards Panel (HITSP) and other Standards Development Organizations (SDOs) involved in healthcare information technology and interoperability. He held executive roles at both ambulatory and enterprise vendors. He currently is co-chair of the Board for Integrating the Healthcare Enterprise (IHE) International, representing HIMSS.

In addition to special interests in interoperability, he is passionate about consumer engagement, person-centered care, quality/safety, public policy, and privacy/security.

Dr. Jacob Reider, MD, is the Chief Executive officer at Alliance for Better Health and has led a number of Healthcare Information Technology start-ups aimed at improving health outcomes with better data. He served in the Office of the National Coordinator of Health IT as both Chief Medical Officer and Deputy National Coordinator 2011–2014 and previously was the Chief Medical Informatics Officer for Allscripts. He received his MD from Albany Medical College and did his Family Medicine Residency at St. Clare's Hospital.

Dr. Joseph H. Schneider, MD, is a retired CMIO who consults in informatics and provides care for newborns as a clinical assistant professor with the University of Texas Southwestern in Dallas. He serves on the Child Health Informatics Advisory Committee for the American Academy of Pediatrics (AAP) and is a founding member of the Texas Medical Association's Healthcare Information Technology (HIT) Committee, known for its involvement in promoting usability and safety.

He was co-author of the 2003 Continuity of Care Record standard, an early interoperability approach. He also coauthored the AAP policy on Personal Health Records and authored the #1 AAP Chapter Resolution of 2003, recommending that the AAP take a leadership position in the development of pediatric EHRs.

Dr. Schneider graduated summa cum laude from Emory and has an MBA from Columbia with 15 years of business experience, including managing a startup medical device company. In 2014, he became board certified in Clinical Informatics.

Dr. Schneider is a competitive racewalker but he loves to go on slow walks with his wife and dog. His passions are the families he cares for and the quality, safety, security, and usability of the technology used to help them have healthy lives.

Dr. Amy M. Sitapati, MD, is the chief medical information officer of Population Health at the University of California San Diego Health. She is clinical professor in the Department of Medicine, Division of General Internal Medicine and Department of Biomedical Informatics. Dr. Sitapati is board certified in internal medicine and clinical informatics. She has oversight of analytics and population health initiatives related to UC San Diego's 49 active patient registries which support bulk activities, care management, care gap closure, and identification of risk. Dr. Sitapati's expertise supports the design and creation of systems that deliver improved care, support pay for performance programs, risk contracts, and CMS innovation initiatives.

R. Dirk Stanley, MD, MPH, is a hospitalist, physician informaticist, and CMIO. Originally from Hartsdale, NY, he started working professionally in the software industry during high school and college. After graduating from University of Massachusetts at Amherst, he earned his MPH in epidemiology at New York Medical College and worked for five years as medical data analyst in the QA department at Westchester Medical Center in Valhalla, NY before starting medical school at St. George's University in Grenada. After an Internal Medicine residency in Albany, NY, his IT and data analysis background led him to Cooley Dickinson Hospital in Northampton, MA where he served for eight years as CMIO and practicing hospitalist. In 2010, he won New England HIMSS Physician-of-the-Year; in 2014, he was ABPM board-certified in clinical informatics, and in 2016, he accepted a position as the first CMIO at University of Connecticut Health in Farmington, CT.

Dr. Harris R. Stutman, MD, serves as the chief medical informatics officer at MemorialCare Health System in southern California. He trained as a pediatric infectious disease physician at the Children's Hospitals of Pittsburgh and Oklahoma and has held full-time academic appointments at the Universities of Pittsburgh, Oklahoma and California-Irvine. His research activity focused on the microbiology of cystic fibrosis-related infections and novel antimicrobial chemotherapy. He has authored more than 50 peer-reviewed articles, 40 book chapters, and two handbooks in the fields of infectious disease and informatics. He also served as chief of staff at Miller Children's Hospital in Long Beach.

His career in medical informatics spans 25+ years, including leadership positions with the Medical Information Systems Physician Society, the Computer-based Patient Record Institute and the Association of Medical Directors of Information Systems. He is a long-time member of the American Medical Informatics Association and HIMSS. In addition to current and previous CMIO positions, he worked for six years on the "vendor side," in product management and clinical system design.

His major responsibilities at MemorialCare focus on EHR implementation and optimization as well as addressing clinical decision support, controlled clinical vocabularies and analytical strategies, and leading their meaningful use initiatives.

Chapter 1

The Evolution of the CMIO in America

Raymond Aller and Richard L. Rydell

Contents

The CMIO position is one of the newest executive positions in American healthcare. The creation of this role can be understood as a maturing of the healthcare industry in the United States, especially in the application of IT in the practice of medicine.

Although the term CMIO was not widely used until the late 1990s, and most institutions did not formally appoint anyone to such a post until early 2000, some physicians were performing this role in the 1970s and 1980s, and even in the 1960s. This chapter focuses on those individuals, some of whom are identified, and others who are more generally described, as they wish to remain anonymous. Some institutions achieved success in relying on such talents. Others took them for granted, and suffered a series of failures after driving them away. We cite those examples with which we are most familiar; there are numerous others who could be discussed, but we lack the knowledge and space to do so here.

Those who have practiced the CMIO role have depended heavily on the historic development of clinical informatics as a discipline by such renowned individuals as Lawrence L. Weed, MD, at the University of Vermont in Burlington, who conceived of the problem-oriented medical record, a way of looking at medical information that has provided the underpinnings for all of our work in electronic medical records (EMRs). Similarly, Octo Barnett, MD, and his team at Massachusetts General Hospital (MGH) in Boston had the brilliant insight to understand that medical data had unique characteristics and to conceive the MUMPS (Massachusetts General Hospital Utility Multi-programming System) database structure, alternatively known as M, and related tools (sometimes called associative databases), which have served as the underpinnings for the most successful and widely deployed large-scale medical software programs, such as Veterans Administration's Decentralized Hospital Computer Program (DHCP), Veterans Health Information Systems and Technology Architecture (VistA), EPIC, Sunquest, Medical Information Technology (Meditech), and many others. The most widely installed and successful EMR system in the United States, EPIC, is built on associative database architecture, as it the most long-lasting governmental system, VA's VISTA. Donald W. Simborg, MD, of the University of California at San Francisco, envisioned the need for peer-based communications protocols such as Health Level 7 (HL7), and built early tools to support hospital-wide communication. Roger A. Cote, MD, DSc (Hon), with the SNOMED Committee, developed multiple editions of the Systematized Nomenclature of Medicine beginning in 1976. Thirty years later, this was amalgamated with the British READ codes, and is now SNOMED-CT, the worldwide lingua franca of medical information. Clem McDonald, MD, led the development of real-world interoperability, through protocols (lab communications), semantics (the Logical Observation Identifiers Names and Codes [LOINC] database and universal standard), and reality (the Indiana Health Information Network). We could list dozens more. But these are the subject pioneers—the CMIOs who have created or taken these tools and made them real in their own institutions.

The earliest creation of an organization-wide EMR system was a 1968–1972 experiment funded by the U.S. Department of Health, Education, and Welfare—a collaboration between the Lockheed Corporation, many of whose engineers and programmers had created the U.S. Gemini space program—and El Camino Hospital in Mountain View, CA. Particularly important to the implementation of this EMR tool at El Camino was Dr. Ralph Watson, who truly embodied the position of CMIO decades before anyone used the term.

In order to better understand how physicians, nurses, and others in healthcare were actually using the medical chart and communications tools, a young hospital administrator, Richard L. Rydell, MBA, set up super-eight movie film with a time code at a busy nursing station at El Camino Hospital. With time-lapse recordings, this pioneer was able to discover what clinicians' communications entailed in the daily process of care and, importantly, how long they took in each of the activities. In retrospect, it is remarkable to realize that they were focused on the improvement of the process of workflow and provider communications, which remains to this day one of the most elusive aspects of EMR implementation.

Although the Lockheed (later Technicon) system implemented in El Camino was implemented in several other hospitals over the next two decades (including the Clinical Centers of the National Institutes of Health [NIH]), the time wasn't yet ripe for the widespread deployment of clinical information systems (CISs).

Another example of physician leadership of hospital informatics unfolded beginning in 1980, when a hospital-based physician arrived at a respected 400-bed community hospital

in a coastal California community, and began functioning as
CMIO (without that formal title). He immediately tackled the
challenge of bringing the hospital from a punch-card-based
Burroughs billing system (the only computer in the hospital)
to an array of badly needed clinical and ancillary systems.
Interestingly, his medical and residency training had included
mentoring by Drs. Roger Cote, Octo Barnett, and Don
Simborg, and his early practice was influenced by the work
of Dr. Clem McDonald, such that he had an uncommonly
deep knowledge of clinical informatics. Beginning in 1980,
he organized site visits, and encouraged system evaluations.
From 1983 to 1985, he guided the technical and clinical
staff of the hospital to selection and installation of several
clinical information systems, including laboratory, radiology,
pharmacy, and patient care/clinical. By 1985, the hospital
was nationally recognized for the excellence of its array of
clinical information systems. Baxter Corporation pointed out
to hospital administrators that the hospital now had the most
complete clinical implementation of the Dynamic Control/
Delta order entry/results reporting system in the United States.
Unfortunately, hospital administration repeatedly refused to
reflect any compensation for the time of their de facto CMIO
in their regular (management-fee) payments to his medical
group. Although his partners made it clear that they couldn't
continue to permit him to work on tasks "that we are not
being paid for," hospital administration obstinately refused to
designate a portion of that payment for clinical informatics,
steadfastly insisting that it wasn't necessary to pay, and they
weren't required to pay for informatics services.

Subsequently, the physician moved his practice to another
city. The community hospital, lacking physician informatics
guidance, went on to purchase a costly and disastrous failure
of a system for physician outreach. A few years later, the
hospital was a major participant in one of the most notable
and spectacular regional health information organization
(RHIO) failures on record.

Decades later, the hospital has recognized that physician informatics expertise is valuable, and they have begun paying a medical staff member as CMIO.

A year after leaving the community hospital, this informaticist realized that a major factor in the hospital's failure to consider payment was that informatics was not an ABMS-recognized (and therefore reimbursable) specialty. He presented the need of certification in clinical informatics as a medical specialty to the American Board of Pathology (ABP), and in 1991 the ABP proposed to the American Board of Medical Specialties that a Speciality Certification in Clinical Informatics be established.[1] The ABP then appointed a test committee to create a certification examination. This task proved exceedingly difficult, and it was not until 2005, when other specialities of medicine joined the work of defining the scope and creating the questions that the exam began to take shape. The first certification examination in clinical informatics was administered in 2013, and has been administered yearly since then. Practitioners who can show experience in clinical informatics will be grandfathered into be exam-eligible for a few more years. The primary mode of certification will be via a 2-year ACGME-approved fellowship.

Fortunately, other community hospitals took an opposite approach. In 1982, Bill Bria, MD, a pulmonary specialist who had trained at MGH, joined the pulmonary division at Baystate Medical Center in Springfield, MA. Finding that the mainframe computer used there was useless—five years after implementation, its only clinical function was to order chest x-rays—Bria introduced the subject of its inefficiency, with indignation, at a medical staff meeting, putting into motion the dynamic that when one brings up issues, he or she is then charged with finding the solution.

News of his criticism reached the new Chief Information Officer (CIO) at Baystate, Richard Rydell, who also learned of Bria's (successful) Apple II programming course for physicians. At their first meeting, Rydell's opener to Bria was "Would you

6 ■ *The CMIO Survival Guide*

like to do something about the problem you've identified, or
do you want to just continue to complain?"

After consultation with the Chief of Staff and Chief of
Pulmonary, Bria accepted Rydell's challenge to dedicate
25 percent of his work time and salary in order to take on the
challenge as a physician champion in the information services
department. Within a year, this dedicated time increased
to 50 percent, and under Rydell's direction, Bria traveled
throughout the United States, speaking about and beginning
to understand what this task was really about.

Needless to say, Baystate has had far greater and sustained
success than the shortsighted hospital discussed in the
previous example.

1n 1990, the Chief Executive Officer (CEO) of Long Beach
Memorial Medical Center (Long Beach, CA) had decided to
bring in the Technicon system (described earlier) because
of its emphasis on the value of direct physician order entry
(a dozen years before this became fashionable). He brought
in Rich Rydell as CIO, because of Mr. Rydell's experience in
that deployment, who in turn identified a highly respected
member of the medical staff, Harris Stutman, MD, to serve as
CMIO (although the term wasn't in use at that time). Additional
physicians were recruited, all on a part-time basis (including
the informaticist from the first hospital above), and within a
few years the hospital had launched TDS7000, with a rate
of computerized physician order entry (CPOE) as high as
80 percent in some specialties.

There are a number of examples of academics heavily
involved in medical informatics in the 1970s and 1980s. In a
few cases, they functioned as CMIOs, guiding hospital efforts
in systems deployment, and in other instances, they focused
on research and had little or no contact with the clinical side.

Most notable are those who stepped forward and
developed clinical systems that became the core applications
in their academic medical centers. One of the first was
Octo Barnett, MD, founder and Senior Scientific Director

of the Laboratory for Computer Science for over 40 years (retired in 2012). As mentioned earlier, his most far-reaching innovation was to lead the invention in the late 1960s of the MUMPS programming language, which was used to create a clinical laboratory information system, a radiology system, a medication ordering system (decades before its time), a surgical pathology system (that served as a prototype for many of the systems popular today),[2] a Computer Stored Ambulatory Record (precursor of today's EHRs), and many other clinically relevant tools.

At Indiana University's Regenstrief Institute, Clem McDonald, MD, and his team began creating the EHR tool that became the core application for the Wishard Hospital and many other applications. An even more important part of Dr. McDonald's role was in his creation and championing of standards crucial for our interconnected world—the ASTM/HL7 (American Society for Testing and Materials and Health Level 7) standard for reporting observations, and the LOINC standard for naming lab results. Since 2007, he has been leading the Lister Hill Center of the National Library of Medicine.

At the University of Utah LDS Hospital, Homer Warner, MD, PhD, and his team built a series of clinical tools, encapsulated in the HELP system, that became the beacon for such understanding (and application) as how to improve patient outcomes with informatics tools. In the early 1970s, they also constructed the Medlab laboratory information system, one of the first widely installed (and highly functional) laboratory information systems. Unfortunately, the adage that "a prophet is without honor only in his own country" applied to that team. For all the success they had at LDS Hospital (and subsequently at Intermountain Health Care), their opinions and guidance were often disregarded at the "official" University Hospital across town.

At another Harvard Hospital, Beth Israel, Warner Slack and Howard Bleich, both MDs, led their team to create a complete suite of clinical applications, initially deployed in the early 1980s and still in use today. These served as models for the clinical applications subsequently developed at Brigham and Women's Hospital that served for some years as the primary system for Partner's Healthcare.

In 1976, the University of California, San Francisco (UCSF) hired Donald W. Simborg, MD, as their CIO. Not only was it highly unusual to hire a physician for such a post, but this appointment occurred in what proved to be a highly propitious time. Dr. Simborg proceeded to develop a series of applications for important clinical functions (such as patient master index, surgical pathology, etc.) but also came to recognize the most fundamental needs for technical interoperability. It was out of this experience that he founded Simborg Systems and developed the first set of tools to freely interchange clinical data among disparate systems. Simborg's experience was one of the most important factors leading to the creation of the HL7 data interchange standard. In this instance, not only did Dr. Simborg's contributions benefit the patients at UCSF, but UCSF contributed to all of our ability to interchange clinical data.

So, several academic informatics programs became involved clinically, or built applications that became core to their medical center, while others remained preoccupied with academic research projects and largely oblivious to the mission of the medical center they inhabited. To differentiate these two tendencies, one need only consider how many applications developed by that group are being widely applied for patient care in their own institution, or in others.

In other academic institutions, physicians sometimes took the lead in acquiring and implementing commercial systems. One of the most notable was Mel Bernstein, MD's comprehensive installation of Meditech applications in 1980 at the University of British Columbia at Vancouver. Dr. Bernstein's vision of an integrated solution serving multiple departments off a single database was an inspiration to many.

Several physicians have assumed key roles in the development of the Veterans Administration's (VA) Decentralized Hospital Computer Program (DHCP), referred to earlier, which evolved to the VistA system. This was for several years generally recognized as the most comprehensive and effective medical information system in the United States.

The history of the evolution of the CMIO in the United States is largely a matter of oral tradition. And in recognizing this, we would be delighted if readers would contribute to us the stories of others who were early pioneers in demonstrating the value of physicians guiding the clinical information strategy of medical centers.

Bibliography

1. Aller RD. Clinical informatics as a medical subspecialty. *Healthc Inf Manage* 1993;7(4):11–16.
2. Aller RD, Robboy SJ, Poitras JW et al. Computer assisted pathology encoding and reporting system. *Am J Clin Path* 1977;68:715–720.

Chapter 2

A CMIO's Perspective from 2018 and Beyond

Pam Arlotto and Howard M. Landa

Contents

When Chief Medical Information Officers (CMIOs) compare notes, their roles may be as different as the organizations they work with—some are the lone voice for informatics within one health system, others lead large informatics teams across multiple partnerships and geographies, and still others support commercial companies. Some CMIOs are focused on electronic health record implementation and optimization, while others are making their mark in analytics, interoperability, care management platforms, and consumer engagement technologies. No longer does "one size fits all" in defining the responsibilities and accountabilities of the CMIO. Yet, regardless of their focus, CMIOs all share great passion for the value health information technology (HIT) and data can bring to the practice of medicine. Each brings an expectation that it make a difference for patients as the industry transitions from fee for service to value-based care.

The focus of this book is for you, the CMIO, who has a vision for change. This book is developed to help each CMIO achieve success while avoiding the obstacles the American medical culture and the complexity of today's healthcare industry can put in your way. Many agree that HIT can fundamentally transform clinical processes, and the team members and organizations that support them. An even greater opportunity exists in managing the outcomes and quality of care for those with chronic disease, preventing at-risk patients from moving to higher risk conditions, and keeping the well healthy for as long as possible. While these are lofty goals, individual CMIOs will have to blaze their own trail, build their own credibility base, and craft their own plan of action for success as it pertains to their unique situation and organization.

We will describe some of the key characteristics and accomplishments that define the CMIO journey, point out some of the "time-honored" pitfalls, and introduce the emerging trends that will shape the field in the years to come. While no perfect path exists, and a variety of medical cultures exist within academic, health system, community practice, etc., effective CMIOs will need a deep understanding and appreciation of lessons learned from those who preceded them, the impact of local history and personalities, as well as new skills and competencies that are separate from those that served you in clinical practice. Whether new to the position, preparing to take the role to the next level, or serving as a seasoned, long-term informatics leader; successful CMIOs should demonstrate five characteristics: (1) Vision, (2) Leadership, (3) Planning, (4) Value Communication and Delivery, and (5) Perseverance.

Vision

In the past informatics was relegated to automating and administering existing clinical processes (Reid et al. 2005). When introduced in 2011, Meaningful Use (MU) was focused on increasing the adoption of electronic health records (EHRs) by physicians and hospitals. By 2015, 89% of U.S. hospitals and 87% of office-based physicians had implemented EHRs (http://www. dashboard.healthit.gov/). The third and final stage will focus on advanced use of these systems during 2018 and transition into the Merit-based Incentive Payment System (MIPS) program established by the Medicare Access and CHIP (Children's Health Insurance Program) Reauthorization Act. This regulatory push set the stage and established the foundation for digitized clinical information and restructured clinical processes. For some, without the "check the box" rigor of the MU program, the path forward has become less clear. The good news is that a foundation is in place based on the work of several generations of applied medical informatics pioneers. This history is summarized in medical informatics literature, in the previous version of this book, and through countless presentations at healthcare industry conferences. The challenge, for each of you, is that each medical setting has its own unique set of variables and can be influenced by market progress toward value-based care; the readiness of clinicians for change; the skillsets and resources dedicated to HIT, Informatics, Analytics and Quality; and a variety of other factors. Each CMIO will need to grasp and communicate the potential value of the change and required investment, and inspire colleagues, executives, and patients alike. Vision alone is never enough; without it, you will be lost in the detail and complexity of the task.

Leadership

The American medical profession has, over the past 50 years, significantly changed; from an early focus on

community-based primary care to increasing levels of
specialization and intervention. Medical technology and
pharmaceutical advances have brought new options in
treatment. Opportunities to test and perform procedures
are endless, yet third party payers exert an ever-increasing
pressure on medical professionals to reduce the cost of
care. The sea of change that is upon the healthcare industry
brings with it consolidation of health systems, practice
acquisition and physician employment, new structures and
organizational models (i.e., clinical integration networks,
accountable care organizations, patient centered medical
homes, etc.); new reimbursement agreements; changing care
models, and more. Driven by the recognition that chronic
disease, an aging population, and the quality chasm (IOM
2001) cannot be solved in today's fragmented delivery
system, the patient–doctor relationship is changing. The
traditional encounter-based health system where a patient
presents with an illness, is diagnosed, and receives treatment
before exiting the system is being augmented with a more
longitudinal approach. New team-based clinical decision-
making approaches will emphasize prevention and wellness
while simultaneously managing the ongoing care of patients
with multiple chronic conditions as they traverse the care
continuum—from ambulatory to acute to postacute and
often across competing health systems. HIT will enable
new capabilities at the health system, organizational, and
individual levels. Creation of a digital, connected, patient-
centered health and healthcare ecosystem will require
visionary leaders. For you, the CMIO, this sea-change
presents unprecedented opportunity.

Planning

The Triple Aim Institute for Healthcare Improvement (IHI)
can serve as the guidepost for planning the journey to

high value healthcare as well as the role of HIT in the transformation. Goals for improved patient experience of care (including quality and satisfaction); the improved the health of populations; and reduction in the per capita cost of healthcare establish a clear direction for leaders as they plan. As the industry transitions to manage the health of populations and is reimbursed for the assumption of risks, information systems that engage consumers, patients, and care delivery teams in new and different ways will proliferate. The traditional clinical decision-making process, professional roles, and clinician autonomy will be challenged. CMIOs initially focused on EHR adoption, which were originally designed to support clinical documentation of the encounter. Today, many CMIOs serve as a convener, a collaborative partner, and steward of change. They work to:

■ Harvest data to create actionable insights that inform the clinical decision-makers
■ Incorporate clinical decision support tools and point of care dashboards
■ Design new workflows, optimize the systems to incorporate care management processes and build longitudinal plans of care
■ Explore telehealth, home-based monitoring, and other patient centered technologies

Planning for meaningful change will require, you the CMIO, to become adept at balancing the needs or demands of health system executives, clinical colleagues, and the patient with the available resources. Your planning process should (1) clarify the goals or objectives to be achieved, (2) formulate strategies to achieve them, (3) define an integrated plan (i.e., people, process, data, technology, and level of change desired), (4) engage key stakeholders and responsible parties, and (5) stage and monitor the sequence of activities as appropriate.

Communication of Value

Most CMIOs have heard the story of the introduction of the stethoscope and the quotation that appeared in *The Times Newspaper of London* in 1834, "That it will ever come into general use, notwithstanding its value, is extremely doubtful; because its beneficial application requires much time and gives a good bit of trouble both to the patient and the practitioner; because its hue and character are foreign and opposed to all our habits and associations" (Forbes 1834). A similar quotation illustrates both a challenge and the opportunity for the CMIO, "Health Informatics is as much about computers as cardiology is about the stethoscope" (Coiera 1995). Many CMIOs still find confusion within their organizations regarding their role, purpose, and ultimate value. Long known as the "doctor in IT," CMIOs are often associated with the work of the Information Technology department and medical informatics. Adding to the confusion is the expansion of informatics roles within nursing, pharmacy, quality, imaging, research, and other disciplines. As the need for transformational change becomes more apparent, an opportunity exists for CMIOs to align the work of these disciplines as *Health Informatics (HI)*. Communicating the value of HI goes beyond traditional systems adoption and optimization to contributions to the enterprise strategy and the design of new care management platforms to support this strategy. As the CMIO, you are uniquely qualified to articulate the quantitative as well as qualitative benefits, help assess the risks, define the alignment of the enterprise direction and IT investment, and analyze the potential return on the investment of the change. It is preeminently important that the CMIO be recognized as a physician first and foremost, and as such, a defender of patient safety and quality of care. The successful CMIO will also be able to bridge this viewpoint with a value story that resonates with the clinical, administrative, financial, and strategic perspectives of the organization.

Perseverance

"Meaningful Use" incentives certainly accelerated the acquisition and implementation of EHRs in hospitals and practices across the country. At the same time, technology and the internet-of-things is disrupting business models in retail, transportation, financial services, and other industries. A decade ago, Apple launched its iPhone and the mobile revolution, leaving few untouched. While the rate of change in healthcare has seemed glacial at times, steady persistence for the CMIO is critical. Next generation HIT systems will be fundamentally different. They will be patient-centered and serve as a hub for the care team. They will be highly configurable with multiple ways to input data, including patient participation in notes and elements of their history. Data will be external and shareable across the continuum, and the user-friendly systems will be designed to promote health, manage care activities, and support clinical decision-making. In the short term, each CMIO must set expectations with leadership and his/her colleagues regarding a long-term commitment to change and workflow redesign—as well as the value of information (collection, analysis, and reporting). Establishing a governance and quality improvement process for data and information should be a primary responsibility of the CMIO, and directly connect you to the Chief Medical Officer, Chief Information Officer, Chief Quality Officer, and others in leadership.

References

Coiera E. 1995. Medical informatics. *British Medical Journal*, 310(6991): 1381.
Forbes J. *The Times Newspaper of London*. 1834. https://quoteinvestigator.com/2012/06/15/stethoscope-doubtful/

Institute of Medicine (IOM). *Crossing the Quality Chasm: A New Health System for the 21st Century.* Washington, DC: National Academy of Sciences, 2001.

Reid PP, Compton WD, Grossman JH, Fanjiang G, editors. *Building a Better Delivery System: A New Engineering/Health Care Partnership.* Washington, DC: National Academies Press, 2005.

Chapter 3

CMIO, CMIO 2.0, and the CHIO

Pam Arlotto

Contents

Pursuit of high-value healthcare is the common strategic theme for most health systems, physician groups, and payers today. With variations on timing and pace of change, most prioritize strategic growth, clinical integration, and increased attention on population health. While there isn't a "one size fits all solution," it is clear that the current fee-for-service model incentivizes volume of services over quality of care and improved outcomes. The industry has begun the shift with Medicare as the largest payer in healthcare leading the way, with Medicare Advantage, Medicare Shared Savings Programs, Next Generation Accountable Care Organizations (ACOs), bundled payments, and a variety of alternative payment models. For the CMIO, it is important to understand the implications of this shift to your organization, its strategy, and the required investment in HIT to support the transition.

The following framework may help clarify the shift (Figure 3.1).

It is important to note that the timeline for each stage varies based on market conditions, the reimbursement contracts with payers, the level of clinical integration, and the health system's preparedness through development of a value-driven HIT infrastructure. New Care Management Platforms will integrate EHRs across the continuum through interoperability, analytics, care management, and patient/consumer engagement modules. The CMIO will play a key role in designing these highly configurable platforms for value, so they will:

- Improve point of care decision-making through clinical decision support
- Stratify patients with specific conditions and track disease status

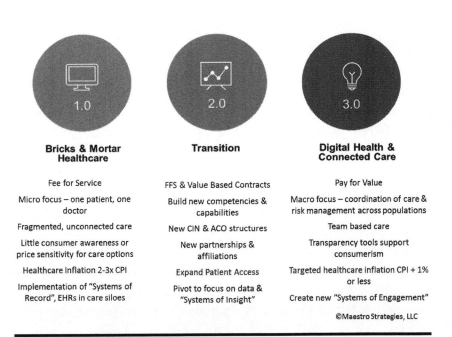

Bricks & Mortar Healthcare	Transition	Digital Health & Connected Care
Fee for Service	FFS & Value Based Contracts	Pay for Value
Micro focus – one patient, one doctor	Build new competencies & capabilities	Macro focus – coordination of care & risk management across populations
Fragmented, unconnected care	New CIN & ACO structures	Team based care
Little consumer awareness or price sensitivity for care options	New partnerships & affiliations	Transparency tools support consumerism
Healthcare Inflation 2-3x CPI	Expand Patient Access	Targeted healthcare inflation CPI + 1% or less
Implementation of "Systems of Record", EHRs in care siloes	Pivot to focus on data & "Systems of Insight"	Create new "Systems of Engagement"

©Maestro Strategies, LLC

Figure 3.1   Transition from volume to value.

- Improve access and care management across geographic and time differences
- Integrate data across multiple entities, processes, and functions
- Improve communications across care teams and transitions of care
- Measure and analyze performance of care for individuals and populations

The remaining sections of this chapter describe the evolution of the CMIO's role and responsibilities at each stage in the transition.

Bricks and Mortar Healthcare

A typical CMIO 1.0 is focused on adoption of the EHR within one entity—hospital or health system. They often report to the Chief Information Officer and are sometimes known as the "doctor" in IT. They are valued as an influencer across the organization but rarely have staff reporting to them. Often organizational uncertainty exists regarding the role, its value, and differentiation from IT. Many new CMIOs find themselves becoming reactive, responding to multiple requests, with little time to plan. 1.0 CMIOs have limited budgetary authority. C-Suite business practices are often foreign and the tendency to fall back on "fix it now" problem-solving approaches that served them so well in their clinical practices. While there will always be a need for informaticists to focus on adoption and optimization of the EHR, if the organization is transitioning to 2.0, a game plan for the transition to CMIO 2.0, developed in concert with other senior leaders will further clarify priorities. Important components of this plan include:

- Clear messaging regarding the Vision and Guiding Principles of Health Informatics and Analytics within the enterprise

- A defined Health Informatics Strategy that spells out informatics and analytics strategic imperatives and critical success factors
- A clear, multiyear operating model that explains:
  - The relationship of the CMIO in relation to other C-Suite executives such as the Chief Information Officer, Chief Clinical Officer, Chief Transformation Officer, Chief Innovation Officer, etc.
  - The role of Health Informatics and Analytics in convening and consulting with other disciplines in addition to having primary responsibility for specific core activities in data definition, collection, exchange, aggregation, analysis, and use
  - The difference/similarities in corporate Informatics and Analytics versus local "at-the elbow" informatics roles
  - A resource plan that identifies skills, capabilities, and gaps in competencies
- Tools and measurement techniques for value realization and return on investment analyses
- In many cases, a personal development plan for the CMIO, one that expands leadership, strategic, and business knowledge

Transition

The 2.0 CMIO is aligned with and often reports to Clinical leadership—the Chief Medical Officer, Chief Clinical Officer, Chief Transformation Officer, or Chief Integration Officer—often with a dotted line reporting relationship to the CIO. At this stage, the attention of the CMIO must "pivot" from a focus on EHR adoption to people, process, information, and change—or value realization. Responsibility expands beyond acute care to the continuum and to affiliates and partners. Analytics and insight-driven decision-making becomes increasingly important as the organization experiments with new care delivery models and launches clinical integration networks and accountable care organizations. The role of the CMIO 2.0 is more formal, more structured, and more strategic. According to William F. Bria, Board Chair of AMDIS, "the next generation CMIO will be a bit of a scientist, quality officer and leader of strategic change." These CMIOs will have broader responsibilities for change and value, leading teams of informaticists, process engineers, data analysts, content management specialists, and change management specialists to redesign processes, improve data integrity, educate clinicians and senior leaders, develop point of care decision support, and hardwire quality into clinical workflows.

Digital Health and Connected Care

The CMIO 3.0 leader has to master 1.0, 2.0, and emerging care models for 3.0. As the organization takes on risks and develops provider-led population health management strategies, some assume the title Chief Health Information Officers (CHIOs) and lead the convergence of quality, informatics, and analytics. Others continue to use the title CMIO, while others serve as Chief Medical Officers, Chief Transformation or Innovation Officers, leaders of Population Health Management, or are Chief Information Officers. Regardless of the title, a number of consistent patterns are apparent, the CHIO or senior clinician with responsibility for health information is focused on:

■ Leading information strategy and governance
■ Ensuring digital capabilities are woven into the fabric of new business, care delivery, and reimbursement models and service can be delivered anytime, anywhere
■ Getting the right information to the right person at the right time to make the right decision to create value

- Harnessing the power of big data, building capabilities in predictive and prescriptive management of populations, and personalized medicine
- Thinking systematically about the health system as a whole instead of specific components, considering emerging trends and opportunities for innovations
- Leading design of the digital patient experience, considering the role of patient/family generated data, exploring the use of social media and stratified health information to improve wellness, prevention and management of chronic disease as well as retail health, virtual health, and other new methods of health delivery
- Partnering with payers and other health systems to bend the cost curve while simultaneously improving quality

The CHIO, a member of the C-Suite, collaborates with other leaders to drive the transformation to value-based care. There is less focus on who reports to who and dotted line reporting relationships associated with 2.0.

As the transformation of healthcare accelerates, and our care delivery platforms are digitized; physician leadership of Health Informatics, Analytics, and Quality will become more critical. These physician leaders will ensure that the complex decisions associated rethinking delivery models to bend the cost curve and improve outcomes, consider tradeoffs and practical realism needed to ensure value from our investment in HIT.

Chapter 4

Designing an Effective Informatics Organizational Structure

Sameer Badlani

Contents

The rapidly evolving role and stature of the executive role of CMIO/CHIO often comes with budgetary responsibility and direct oversight of personnel, creating the opportunity to design and influence informatics and IT organization structures. Refining an existing or building a new informatics organizational structure is one of the most tangible and vital undertakings for the CMIO/CHIO role and branding. In this chapter, the four basic guiding principles of organizational design are discussed. I have found these to be useful, educational, and perhaps essential.

The experience of designing and building an effective informatics organization is often akin to the much used analogy of building a plane while flying it. Therein lies the challenge and adventure of this very meaningful endeavor. No matter how big or small your groups in terms of Full Time Equivalent (FTE) counts, the impact of a well-functioning group is far reaching, especially as a significant proportion of the work in informatics will always be done through influence. Making the sum of your contributors count more than the individual parts is the objective. This is at no time a plug and play exercise. The ability to lead and execute nimbly rests with the design and management of the organizational structure. While regular adjustments are expected and beneficial, the basic template has tremendous impact on the delivery of value.

The *first principle* is to use the goals and purpose of your informatics organization as the North Star. It is important to define the rationale for creating an organizational structure before delving into the kinds of organization structures and associated strategies. The obvious one is you have a team and you need to organize the members into functional units and optimize the number of direct reports you and your direct reports manage.

Not surprisingly, the current thinking in organizational structure relies heavily on decades of organizational development research focused on behavior, productivity, and creativity. This has led to the paradigms of hierarchy and functional schemas to be superseded by the goals of communication, empowerment, and productivity as the main drivers.

As early as 1974, Peter F. Drucker, the father of modern management, noted in his article on "New Templates for Today's Organizations" that "Ideally, an organization should be multiaxial, that is, structured around work and task, *and* results and performance, *and* relationships, *and* decisions."[1]

Deliberately avoiding the trap, or rather the easy option, and replicate existing templates of organizational structures that are expressed in your native environment is the second guiding principle. You may choose as a nuanced diplomat to start close to what surrounds you but the foundation and design should always be to push the cultural limits and create a purpose-oriented team that is focused on value generation and not just be content with reporting structures and hierarchy. The effectiveness and branding of a forward thinking informatics group cannot be built on organizational templates from the 1960s. All informatics executives need to ask themselves, "What benefit are we aiming to bring to the organization; what is the indispensable value proposition of informatics to the enterprise?"

The *second principle* deals with the kind of organizational structure to choose from. The three major thematic designs are hierarchical, matrix, and flatter (not flat) with a focus on networks of teams. In the 2016 Deloitte Consulting article on organizational design, the concept of "networks of teams" is highlighted with a focus on strong communication, rapid information flow, and empowerment.[2]

The hierarchal structure was predominantly top down and one-way communication design. Recognition of the inherent challenges in this dysfunctional model flattening was undertaken with the aim of creating the next iteration, which is called the Matrix organization. This came from a desire to "flatten" the organization structure. Majority of companies have gotten rid of the top down and favor the Matrix template with fewer layers, hence a flatter structure. Unfortunately, while well intentioned the matrix structure often became the catchall for the nonhierarchical templates and led to even more confusion and disorganization.

Described quite bluntly by Gill Corkindale in her 2011 article on "The importance of Organizational Design and Structure," she says "Often, I see little more than a traditional hierarchy flattening out, perhaps broadening into a matrix structure in parts of the organization. More often than not, though, the hierarchy remains embedded in the "new" structure, which can cut across its effectiveness and leave people confused. Worse, organizations rarely show people how to operate in a new structure, which can also undermine effectiveness."[3]

After evaluating trends seen across various businesses and startup cultures, the concept of flatter structure with intent for "network of teams" design seems to be the most popular in modern management discussions. This template is focused around a specific product or service with multidisciplinary teams working together towards a common goal. In healthcare, this is most evident in the service line concept even though the successful implementations are not as "flat" in comparison to other industries.

Healthcare presents unique challenges and perhaps an unparalleled opportunity in creating a nimble yet purposeful cross-functional team that includes clinicians (nurses and physicians), business analysts, researchers, and administrators to name a few. Combinations of such multitalented individuals are present in almost all organizations, irrespective of their geography and size.

In the 2013 HBR article "The Strategy That Will Fix Healthcare," Michael E. Porter and Thomas H. Lee, MD discuss the concept of Integrated Practice Units designed to provide a focused area of service to the patients as the roadmap for value in healthcare.[4] Such focused delivery teams look beyond the hierarchical reporting structure and embrace the team concept designed around a focused service model. While reporting structure still has a need in the workplace for talent management and development, they should not define how coworkers engage in execution.

The field of informatics lends itself delightfully well to the concept of service lines with Electronic Health Record applications, data-analytics, variation reduction, and efficiency-training as potential "teams." This template for organizational design and processes with an aim towards value generation is also a leading concept in the Information Technology Infrastructure Library for Information Technology Service Management (ITSM), first conceptualized in the 1980s by the

United Kingdom government.[5] This concept has gone through multiple iterations over the years while retaining the basic premise of service delivery, not function, as the focus area.

Focus on removing unnecessary levels of hierarchy in your organization with hybrid reporting structures. Create delivery-oriented teams and a structure that allows for individual contributors (who may not be good managers of people, but good team players) to succeed. This rounds up the second design principle.

The *third principle* is of design fit or validity. While you may often have a distinct notion of your design, you may most likely find that the organization is not ready for such a radical (or even any) change. Do you have the talent to fill all the roles you need for your agile organization? For all you know, your design may not be a good fit for the goals you have penned down after reading the first principle, or even from the job description for which you were hired.

Thinking through the following questions will allow you to develop a better understanding of the current state of the informatics team and develop an action plan to remain effective and lead proactively while trying to succeed at cultural change management. This discussion is influenced and partially adopted from "Do You Have a Well-Designed Organization?" by Michael Goold and Andrew Campbell.[6]

1. Does your design allow for sufficient management attention to maintain a focus and agility? When your senior managers also have the responsibility to execute tactics and contribute to strategy, getting a sense of the individual's management style and balancing that with "doing" is probably a weekly balancing act. People management is a full-time job in itself sometimes.
2. Have you taken the time to evaluate the strengths, motivations, and weaknesses of your people? When a structure does not function, it is natural to blame the people but not realize the design was not in tune with the

people on your team. This analysis is not trivial, comes with time, and requires constant pondering and redesign.

3. Do you have effective controls to exercise accountability? This is probably the most important consideration next to communication. Being able to prioritize, evaluate progress, and hold teams and individuals accountable are essential for success. Using key performance indicators and defining metrics that are meaningful are basic building blocks for accountability. Measure, measure, and measure again.

4. Is your template feasible? Depending on your state laws and organizational policies hiring physician informaticians who still practice (a trait I consider essential to success) may not be straightforward. Often clinicians in traditional applications roles may be the best informaticists in your organization but moving them can be impeded not just by politics but the gap that they will leave behind in their legacy roles. Then there is the conundrum of part-time roles. While very common in informatics, it should be seen and leveraged as a strategic advantage.

The final and *fourth principle* deals with essentials of communication, branding, and collaboration (internal and more importantly external to your department). Let us assume you have designed the ideal fit template for your organization within the larger enterprise and have the right individuals in the appropriate roles. Much work still needs to be done; take a deep breath.

Essentially, all organizational redesign efforts are initiated with recognition of the communication challenges the current design and human behaviors have fostered. Think through the mechanism, cadence, and mode of information flow from you, through your management team, and most importantly and essentially, back to you. The concepts of Daily Engagement Systems are increasingly popular in high-reliability organizations looking to leverage Lean mindset or the Lean Daily Management system.[7] In many clinical delivery sites, daily safety and quality huddles are now considered best practice. This is an excellent example of making your communication part of the structure.

Next is branding, and in my opinion, it probably deserves its own chapter in the next edition of this book. While many eloquent definitions can be easily found with a simple online search, to me it can be best summed up as intentional activities, often repetitive, with a goal to connect with your consumers and team members at an intellectual and emotional level to create a widely understood and common understanding of your value proposition and excellence in execution. These are not limited to marketing, logos or even mission statements.

Delivering consistent value in the eye of your consumer in a timely and cost-effective manner is the most meaningful branding exercise that you—as the executive—can focus on. Additional and again intentional activities include:

■ Consistent talking points for your management layer created with their engagement
■ Sharing the story of your team's contributions in ways that resonate with your organization's value proposition
■ Obsessive focus on measurement and transparency

Finally, let's discuss the need and pitfalls of collaboration. As we build our network of teams, it is essential to recognize that the team will and should have external contributors to your organization. Again, pressure test your organizational template to ensure it supports, promotes, and celebrates collaboration. No single department has all the talent needed for successful execution. In fact, external contributors often serve the dual purpose of subject matter expertise (that is not existent in your domain) and to act as mirrors for your best thought-out ideas.

This has to be balanced by collaboration overload and a consensus paralysis, which is probably the most visible dysfunction of matrixed organizations. Clear lines of accountability and responsibility help. Frequent check-in and realistic deadlines are essential project management traits that need to be hardwired. This concludes the fourth and potentially the most essential principle of effective organizational design.

I do not consider any of the above principles to be either absolute or to be executed in any particular order. As noted earlier, you will never get the luxury of starting from scratch, having no deliverables due while you perform your analysis, and perhaps—most amazingly—with no personnel crises left for you to deal with. Be decisive, be transparent, and communicate your vision regularly. It may be essential to start on a many of these deliverables simultaneously, and that is perfectly normal. Remember: you signed up for this important leadership role.

While this chapter aims to elucidate and summarize the essential concepts of organizational design that have helped me in my journey, I highly recommend perusing the references below.

References

1. Drucker P. 1974. https://hbr.org/1974/01/new-templates-for-todays-organizations. Accessed September 2017.
2. Deloitte Consulting. 2016. https://dupress.deloitte.com/content/dam/dup-us-en/articles/human-capital-trends-introduction/DUP_GlobalHumanCapitalTrends_2016_4.pdf. Accessed September 2017.
3. Corkindale G. 2011. https://hbr.org/2011/02/the-importance-of-organization. Accessed September 2017.
4. Michael EP, Thomas HL. 2013. https://hbr.org/2013/10/the-strategy-that-will-fix-health-care. Accessed September 2017.
5. Wikipedia. "ITIL." https://en.wikipedia.org/wiki/ITIL. Last modified September 10, 2017.
6. Goold M, Campbell A. 2002. https://hbr.org/2002/03/do-you-have-a-well-designed-organization. Accessed September 2017.
7. Timpson J. 2015. https://www.linkedin.com/pulse/lean-daily-management-system-using-structure-engage-optimize-timpson. Accessed September 2017.

Chapter 5

The CMIO's Relationship with the Physician Community

Harris R. Stutman

Contents

In previous editions of this book, the emphasis has been on the CMIO role in (1) working primarily with physicians in (2) a traditional hospital-based medical staff within (3) an organization planning to implement a robust, comprehensive set of electronic health record (EHR) solutions. In almost all circumstances, this is no longer the case. Hence, this chapter needs to address the world in which the CMIO—or CHIO, in some organizations—now lives, not that of the past. Over the past 5–15 years, most hospitals have transformed themselves

into integrated health delivery networks, which include
something akin to a "credentialed medical staff" but also
include, often at levels of much enhanced importance, a large
group of physicians, physician extenders, and other clinicians
who have much tighter alignment with the organization and
its leadership than in the past. This significantly alters the role,
the responsibilities, and the ability of the CMIO to influence
and effect change, as will be discussed here. Additionally,
although the CMIO title is still more widely filled than that
of other informatics leaders, such as those in nursing (CNIO),
Quality and Performance Improvement (e.g., CQIO), or
Pharmacy (CPIO), and others, working with other clinical
informatics leaders has become a key component of the CMIO
role. Finally, the focus of the modern CMIO is no longer on
the procurement, configuration, or implementation of the
EHR. Indeed, CMS statistics for 2016 show that >99% of all
hospitals—and hence their delivery networks—have adopted
and implemented certified EHR solutions (only 9 states in the
United States have less than 99% adoption and no U.S. state
has less than 96% adoption). Therefore, the focus of clinical
informatics efforts, and that of the CMIO leader has completely
shifted to usability and workflow enhancements, design
optimization, and value realization, the latter often through
increasing collaboration with colleagues in the decision
support and business intelligence domains. The only thing
within this portfolio that has remained relatively unchanged
is the emphasis on communication and change management,
which was and is an integral component of the CMIO's
interactions with his/her physician and clinical colleagues,
whether within or without the medical staff hierarchy.

In the corporate world, a very common question is
"who do you report to?" In clinical medicine, although the
traditional "medical staff" hierarchy has had little use for
such organizational arrangements, it can be an important
attribute of the CMIO role. In the past, power, and more
importantly influence, tended to rest with those physicians

who were the most productive, far enough from residency to be well-seasoned yet still energetic and committed to the world beyond their practices. In today's typically integrated healthcare organization, however, chiefs of medical staff, heads of medical staff departments, and medical directors within the various groupings of an integrated network can be key power figures, with significant capability to impact the success of informatics initiatives and therefore must be included in the sphere of influence of all high-achieving CMIO's.

In any organization, the person you report to, those who you relate to ("dotted lines"), and the specific people who report to you—the reporting hierarchy—are what is important, not specific titles or roles. But again, unlike as happens in clinical medicine, those people frequently change within an administration, and in the experience of many, the direct connection between a title, a role, and the importance of that leader to the success of the CMIO can be ephemeral at best.

The new CMIO is best advised to start out by assuming that roles, responsibilities and power grids align, but be prepared to quickly update that mindset as the true movers and shakers within the clinical hierarchy become apparent. How the CMIO positions himself or herself within the medical organization can thus have a significant impact on success.

Clinical Practice and the CMIO Role

In the past, it has often been perceived that the CMIO's influence and ability to lead in a change management role was highly related to their perception as a credible clinician ("Why should I listen to the recommendations of "just another" administrator about how I do my job, just because he has an MD after his or her name?"). Given the emergence of a cadre of physician leaders, up to the CEO level at the most respected health delivery organizations in the United States, this is no longer universally the case. If the CMIO/physician leader has credibility due to education or academic background, previous experience as a respected clinician within the medical organization, or similar credentials, whether he/she remains in active practice can become "negotiable." There are several aspects of this state of affairs that should be examined.

Part of the characterization of a CMIO includes training as a physician. But having medical credentials is not the same as having the experience of practicing medicine, understanding its workflows and its focus on quality and outcomes; this is what truly separates the CMIO from other individuals in information technology. Not only does such experience enhance the ability to suggest, support, and effect change among physicians, it also enhances the credibility of the CMIO among nonphysician leaders with whom they will work. High-level nonphysician administrators increasingly understand the benefit gleaned from having practiced medicine, especially in an environment relevant to the CMIO position. Although it can clearly be abused, the simple aspect of respect that results in being addressed as "Dr. Smith" rather than "Bill' can carry significant weight. Once the CMIO makes it clear to physician colleagues and leaders and nonclinical leadership that he/she does not simply think that the "MD" title wins every argument, but is committed to a thoughtful data-driven approach to informatics decision-making and EHR optimization, then the clinical credibility can be a very useful adjunct.

As stated, physicians who have not had clinical practice experience bring considerable limitations. With the increasing number of clinical and biomedical informatics programs at the MS and PhD levels, we are seeing more CMIO candidates who have graduated from medical school and immediately gone into graduate programs without even residency experiences. This can be problematic in many circumstances, raising significant barriers to success if others, especially physicians, perceive that an executive without "real" clinical experience is "driving without a license." Those responsible for evaluating CMIO candidates must appreciate that there is simply no way to know, speak or lead on issues related to physician workflows and EHR usability without experience in the practice of medicine. Similarly, understanding and leading initiatives focused on clinical quality and performance improvement, and how IT solutions can assist in its optimization demands a keen understanding of how physicians and their extenders work in the real world. A personal observation would be that training programs alone do not convey such experience, given their dissimilarity to even the employed practice models so common today.

Less commonly, there can also be obstacles to acceptance if there is a clinical background but it has been substantially different from that of those in the environment he or she is entering, such as a physician well schooled in running a private practice who joins a Medicaid-focused health maintenance organization (HMO) as an informatics leader. There can be other considerations such as whether certain, well-circumscribed specialty experiences, say in pediatrics or anesthesiology, prepares an otherwise well-qualified CMIO candidate for a position in an integrated healthcare system. This is especially true if the specialty experience is not seen as a team-building, collaborative one—as is so necessary to the typical CMIO role, but rather a specialty where one practices alone. It is also true that the CMIO must absolutely be seen as having interests being "beyond" his or her own specialty training and focus. Although one cannot ignore one's personal experience, the perception that the CMIO coming from an internal medicine background, for instance, is going to prioritize the optimization of the workflows and informatics capabilities most relevant to that specialty, rather than those related to surgery or pediatrics would be a critical mistake. However, these personality and leadership issues seem likely to be sorted out during the evaluation and interview process and are a much less challenging consideration than the nonpractice one.

If the prospective CMIO plans to continue to maintain a clinical presence, either out of interest or because of perceived credibility advantages, the physician must consider what it means to balance the demands of a physician with the demands of a CMIO. Where will the time come from that is needed to fulfill both roles and do them well?

This leads to one of the key areas of controversy regarding the CMIO role—whether they should continue clinical practice after assuming informatics leadership. The argument is ofttimes made that the responsibilities and expectations of each position are such that maintaining a medical practice requires unacceptable compromises. This argument is most frequently put forth by the recruiters, and in some cases by the employers of CMIOs. There are three significant considerations here.

First, is this something that the prospective CMIO wishes to do? That is a deal breaker in my view. Absent real enthusiasm, the perception that one is going through the motions, attending one half-day family medicine clinic every two weeks, or taking hospitalist call once per month can harm one's credibility more than serve it. And of course, with limits on the number of hours in the workday, and the well-known downsides to multitasking, such "distractions" cannot help but distract from the potential for CMIO success.

Second, does the physician need to do this to attain the "street cred" that is deemed helpful to his or her success in working with a medical community and staff. If the physician is new to the organization, it can be helpful to start with a manageable clinical schedule, perhaps 20%–25% FTE. In this way, the CMIO learns about the organization, its culture, and its workflows in ways that might not otherwise be possible. However, if the physician has been an integral part of the medical community that he/she is about to lead, then this becomes a much less relevant consideration. In this case, the physician's influence and credibility have presumably both become well-established—and been confirmed during the evaluation process—and the most important considerations default to the first one listed above.

Finally, what is the role and job responsibility expectation? Even the busiest, most driven CMIO needs work–life balance. If it is clear that the CMIO responsibilities within the organization will include more than enough activities to occupy a 50–60-hour work week—general C-suite responsibilities, physician governance, and other leadership roles, coordinating with other informatics and medical staff committees and workgroups (PI, PT, CDS, etc.) as well as dealing with day to day informatics decision-making, then some clear-eyed decisions need to be made as to whether the advantages of continuing clinical practice outweigh the obvious drawbacks.

What should not be overlooked, of course, are the advantages provided to the organization by a physician executive who still practices the art for which he or she trained. So, the controversy breaks down into two issues: (1) Does a CMIO come into the position with substantial experience practicing medicine; and (2) Should the CMIO continue/begin a clinical practice in his or her administrative role? There are several benefits that emanate from a CMIO's decision to continue practicing. In the minds of many physicians, what truly defines a physician as such is whether he or she practices. Once a physician ceases to practice, they lose their clinician "cloak" and can become another "suit" to physicians—particularly those who are most change resistant—since they can be labeled as not experiencing the same challenges they may be suggesting are to be imposed on other clinicians. Fairly or unfairly, he or she can be seen as not directly impacted by the operational inefficiencies imposed by imperfectly implemented workflows and insulated from patient or employee complaints arising from poorly designed EHR systems being foisted on them.

Another aspect of this issue that is not frequently addressed is that the successful CMIO can be a risk-taker. Indeed, it is hard to see how any successful CMIO would not embrace the challenges inherent in change management. To create trust, and obtain value, appreciated by all parties—clinical, administrative, and IT staff, he or she will have to take leaps of faith and promote what appear to be unpopular causes. Part of the armor worn by the CMIO is this ability to seamlessly shuttle from clinical to administrative work and back again. This puts him or her in a unique position compared to others in the C-suite. It is a common perception that CMIOs who continue to practice have longer tenure within their organization, compared to other members of the C-suite. The fact that they have existing career options independent of their administrative leadership role may have an important role in that perception.

Let's conclude this consideration of the potential clinical component for the CMIO with a brief mention of three possible scenarios. These are not necessarily mutually exclusive options and may represent an evolving role for a specific CMIO within his or her organization.

The first is when the physician still carries a significant clinical load; 50 percent or more of his or her time being clinical. This often occurs in organizations hiring their first CMIO, looking to recruit someone already on the medical staff who has heretofore served in a physician champion role, and through a mutual understanding, desire to see that role expanded, without a significant change in their clinical workload. It is impossible to conceive that—given the many responsibilities inherent in the modern CMIO role—this can be more than a transitional situation. He/she will not be available for important meetings, and clearly important ad hoc discussions and decision-making will be beyond the pale. In this situation, the CMIO is really still acting as a "physician champion" advising the CMO or CIO. In some cases, despite the title, this might even be considered a traditional (i.e., uncompensated) medical staff position. The situation is inherently not stable over the long run. If the goal of hiring a CMIO is to employ a leader in physician engagement, clinical design, and the optimization of clinical systems, the time commitment will need to be relevant—and obviously such a time commitment will need to be compensated appropriately. A related option might be to apportion the CMIO role among multiple physicians—for example, those with complementary clinical or informatics experiences. For example, there might be a full-time role apportioned equally among a medical/ pediatric-focused clinician and an interventionally-focused one (surgeon, proceduralist, etc.). Or the role might be apportioned among two physicians—one with more technical training and experience in basic informatics and clinical system design, while the other more experienced in the analysis of clinical workflows and communicating with the medical community. This does have potential advantages but requires substantial organization, and the potential of overlap and conflicts in decision-making can be substantial, especially if these physicians bring other dissimilarities to the table (different ages or levels of experience, different level of experience with the specific organization and its culture). However, *if* they can be kept in sync with each other on significant issues, the guarantee that a "CMIO" will be present at the multitude of meetings that benefit from physician informatics involvement could be maximized.

The second scenario is one in which the physician still carries a significant clinical workload, perhaps 25–50 percent. Unfortunately, when the amount of clinical and administrative work is taken together, he or she is usually working far more than those who work exclusively in either clinical medicine or administration. Again, this might work as a transitional situation, with the CMIO time allocation moving gradually toward the third scenario, described below, over a defined time period. Without such a plan, the pull of the dual responsibilities seems likely to inevitably lead to CMIO dissatisfaction, especially given the success-driven personalities of most physicians.

The third common situation—and typically a more sustainable one—is one of a well-defined, constrained practice with the CMIO spending 0.5 to 1.5 days a week practicing clinical medicine. Given the typical 50–60 hour work week of most physicians, this allows the CMIO role to consume a traditional 40-hour work week while maintaining a reasonable workload for the individual. This enables them to maintain a clinical presence and credibility—important for external validity to the broader physician community, while still experiencing the effects of the informatics and EHR-related decision that they are championing in their CMIO role—i.e., internal validity. This option is most available to the nonproceduralist, of course, and may be why, at least at the present, there appears to be an underrepresentation of surgeons and other interventional physicians among the CMIO community.

The CMIO and the Physician Community

Arguably the most important interaction the CMIO has is with the active physician community/medical staff. Those clinicians who are most engaged within the given hospital or delivery network are the ones who will be most impacted by the way that the EHR implementation is planned and implemented, how it is optimized and how the data thereby incorporated within it are used to maximize clinical efficiency, effectiveness, and quality. The CMIO's experience, intelligence, and leadership qualities will be absolutely crucial in this regard. He or she is the lead for change management within the physician community and the level of trust he or she creates as liaison between the physicians, other clinical staff, and the administrative and IT staff will directly relate to the success of his or her change agent role and the organization's success in obtaining value from its IT investments. Unfortunately, it will be impossible to please everyone, so the wise CMIO (another reason to be wary of those without significant experience in a practice context) will appreciate the importance of (1) a vigorous bidirectional stream of communication, (2) an emphasis on change resilience and management, and (3) a willingness to listen to every concern and complaint, while cutting no "secret" deals with those who perceive themselves to be too important to the organization to be asked to follow the same rules as everyone else. These political and administrative skills can often be of greater value to the CMIO's success than an in-depth understanding of user interface design, clinical decision support, and clinical workflow principles. The previous discussion regarding the CMIO's actions and those in the next chapter provide more in-depth discussion and call out specific tools for building these relationships.

Relationship of the CMIO to Other Physician Executives

The CMIO is charged as the key physician leader in the implementation and optimization of EHR and related systems but is also a partner to other physician and nonphysician executive leadership in attaining value from IT investments. To do so, credibility and strong working relationships with medical staff leadership, as well as other physician administrators—e.g., the CMO, the Chief Quality or Performance Improvement Officer (CQO), and other influential practicing physicians is vitally important to being successful in this role. Some of those physician roles and their useful interaction with the CMIO role are described.

The CMIO and Medical Leadership

During the planning for EHR implementation and optimization initiatives in a hospital, medical group, or integrated delivery system, a key predictor of success is the extent to which the interests of the physician community can be fundamentally aligned with the process and goals of the various initiatives. Depending on the characteristics of the healthcare organization, and the specific initiatives—especially those beyond the initial implementation (i.e., those focused in specific areas such as the OR or ED), the responsibility of securing physician buy-in does not fall onto one person or even a few physician leaders, although the CMIO may truly have the most specific interest in helping to assemble a strong core of physician influencers to cover all contingencies.

Supporting Physician Engagement and Communication

A traditionally important ally in this team has been the Chief of the (Hospital) Medical Staff (COS). In almost every hospital, whether academic or community-based, the CMIO must develop a strong working relationship with this elected physician leader and his or her successors. In the evolving integrated delivery system, this role often may have a different title (although COS will be used here) and may even be represented by a near full-time physician administrator akin to the CMIO. A trusting and credible relationship between these physicians and the CMIO can be a natural one, especially if they are as interested and passionate about the potential of healthcare IT in achieving medical staff goals for quality and efficiency. The COS can be an important strategic partner to the CMIO, especially in identifying key physician influencers, subject matter experts to be drawn discussions on clinical content or workflow and preferred avenues of communication.

The successful CMIO will maintain open, and consistent, communication with the COS and leverage this relationship to improve communication with the entire medical staff. This promotes an evolutionary awareness of the challenges with any new feature, function, or workflow and how to make certain these are well understood by all relevant physicians to overcome the traditional reluctance of clinicians to change the ways in which they work. The COS and other members of his or her cabinet can also help align medical staff policies and governance and identify incentives to foster adoption of the system. Although such collaboration is very important during initial implementations, it can also be useful as early decisions are reassessed and changes in content or workflow are made in response to physician suggestions and concerns. Such changes necessarily need to be communicated to physicians as part of a broad ongoing approach to training and education—the nature of which can be optimized with close CMIO collaboration with the COS and similar physician leaders. The successful CMIO will likely want to set up a regular meeting schedule—independent of specific committee or workgroup meetings—with the COS and perhaps other senior physician leadership figures, to stay on the same page, identify common priorities, and make certain that communication is consistently seamless.

Supporting Best Practices and Quality Initiatives

A frequently cited driver for adoption of the advanced EHR is to improve the healthcare organization's ability to both drive and measure quality improvement efforts, whether mandated by external agencies or driven by internal priority goals. Indeed, this is likely to be the single concept around which all clinicians can coalesce in facilitating the significant systemic change effort that EHR implementations posit. In most organizations, there are one or more physician executives who hold primary responsibility to drive the quality agenda forward. Although the title may vary by organization (e.g., Chief Medical Officer, Medical Director for Best Practices, etc.), I will refer to the person or persons fulfilling this role as the Chief Quality Officer (CQO).

As the CQO is responsible for demonstrating organizational performance in the areas of quality and safety, this physician executive should be keenly engaged in adopting technology-based tools that enable robust measurement of clinical process or outcome improvements and hold the potential for optimizing physician decision-making during the course of care. In other words, the CQO is the CMIO's most likely collaborator in identifying and implementing the relevant capabilities of modern data-driven EHR, decision support, and data analytical technologies.

Most CQOs will, therefore, enthusiastically embrace the adoption of IT as a critical foundation for future performance improvement efforts. Since this enthusiasm must be balanced with realistic expectations on how quickly and effectively EHR technology can help affect this change, it is important for the CMIO to manage expectations while working with the CQO to deliver incremental gains to the organization and its stakeholders. Similar to the comments about close collaboration with the COS, the CMIO must establish a strong communication stream with the CQO, while always considering the CQO as a key "customer" whose perspectives must be addressed during each EHR initiative. In many cases, the primary driver for new informatics initiatives is to enhance both the attainment and the documentation of quality improvements such that the CMIO and CQO can be perceived as partners in those initiatives. As an important partner and ambassador of the CQO, the CMIO should help communicate the clinical quality perspectives thoroughly, in parallel to day-to-day project decisions, and assume responsibility for properly guiding EHR project decisions to support existing and future quality priorities.

A CMIO new to an organization should probably spend a significant amount of time early on in developing an understanding of the organizational culture around quality (hopefully evidence-based) as well as existing organizational quality priorities and challenges from the perspective of the CQO.

Focusing on such questions as new informatics initiatives can most usefully address—breadth of agenda, key challenges in terms of data governance and consistency, expectations for new quality programs and how new informatics tools can address them—the CMIO can engage with the CQO and other key leaders to help define a joint expectation of how and within what timeframe the EHR can substantially impact the organization's quality agenda. In that effort, it is important to not oversell the EHR technology as the solution to all organizational challenges surrounding quality or safety but rather as a key tool in the arsenal for quality improvement.

It is relevant in this context to note that many/most such goals will need to engage other nonphysician informatics leaders—those in nursing, pharmacy, performance improvement and research informatics—in order to be successful. Indeed, although beyond the scope of this chapter, it is very relevant to the success of the CMIO that he or she engage such other informatics colleagues in most of his or her efforts. A parochial approach to "physician" informatics—as opposed to a broader one to "clinical" informatics and relevant clinical informatics leadership—will avoid many challenges.

As a representative of the practicing physician community, the CMIO must also be a key negotiator in helping to balance the objective of demonstrating improved quality against the looming challenge of being able to achieve and sustain a massive organizational change incited by technology. Quality initiatives in the pre-HIT era typically were educational and voluntary. With the ability to bring such initiatives, and the tools to address them, right to the point of decision-making and documentation, the amount of workflow disruption and vocal clinician "pushback" can be substantial. Working together with the CMIO, the CQO can and must make it clear to the medical community that such interventions—and interruptions—are not being foisted on them by an uncaring technology, but result from medical leadership's thoughtful use of its new tools to push quality to new levels of achievement.

In the realm of quality improvement, the CMIO, working with the CQO and other leaders, is in an opportune position to spearhead a similar discussion around the timing and extent of EHR-enabled quality improvement and how fast even important, quality-driven change can be implemented. Weighing these considerations and developing a strong governance process involving the CQO, CMIO, and physician leaders must begin early, as there is considerable organizational learning and discussion needed to vet these issues and determine a proper fit with the organization's culture and context.

As these discussions begin and the implementation moves forward, the CMIO has an important responsibility to apply his or her knowledge and experience against the organization's attributes, quality priorities and technical and resource constraints to help support the CQO and other executive and clinical stakeholders in crafting a quality EHR roadmap.

Chapter 6

Healthy Vital Signs: CMIO, CNIO, and Other Informatics Relationships

Joseph H. Schneider

Contents

As informatics grows in importance, some organizations are creating new informatics leadership roles in multiple disciplines. Chief Nursing Informatics Officers (CNIOs) are increasingly common, but roles such as the Chief Research Informatics Officer (CRIO) and Pharmacy Chiefs or Directors of Informatics are also encountered. Other disciplines such as pathology, radiology, rehabilitation, and social work may have formal informatics positions to support and be the voice for clinical technology and processes in their particular disciplines. To be successful, the CMIO needs to understand how to work with these roles and to establish relationships and processes that foster communication and cooperation.

This chapter provides guidance on how the CMIO and these other informatics leaders can work together, whether they are in a single informatics department or a "virtual team" reporting into separate parts of an organization.

The starting point is getting the right people on the team.

Case Study

Healing HealthCare System hired its first Chief Medical Information Officer six years ago after five years of minimal success in implementing an Electronic Medical Record system. The situation that the CMIO faced was not unusual. While lots of good work had been done, informatics governance was in its infancy and informatics leaders other than the CMIO were nonexistent.

Within the first 6 months, the CMIO worked with the Chief Medical and Chief Nursing Officers to hire a CNIO. The CNIO started a program of nursing documentation improvement and developed staff with informatics skills who designed creative tools for nurses and other clinicians. The CMIO often facilitated the CNIOs efforts and the CNIO enabled the CMIO to have a closer relationship with nursing. They performed as a dyad, with the latter staffing the governance committees when the CMIO was not present. The CNIO reported to the CMIO initially, but after 3 years and development of a Nursing Informatics Organization, the CMIO spun off the CNIO position to the CNO to achieve better alignment with nursing.

The CMIO did not stop there; a System Director of Pharmacy Informatics position was created, utilizing a part of the CMIO and Pharmacy Department budget. The Pharmacy Informatics Director reported to the Vice President of Pharmacy but his office was with the other informatics leaders and staff to stay in close communication. This was the start of the CMIO's "virtual team."

In time, another critical position, the System Director of Clinical Decision Support, was created in the Quality Organization with the combined support of the CMIO and the Chief Quality Officer. This person managed the development and maintenance of order sets and protocols in conjunction with the Information Systems Department, which produced the production version of these.

Other shared positions followed as the budget permitted and as the organization's senior leadership understood their importance. Most of the CMIO's "virtual team" reported to him through matrix arrangements. The CMIO's funding and influence provided the "grease and glue" that supported these positions and the people in them. For example, attendance by "virtual team" members at informatics conferences was funded by the CMIO.

The CMIO used several approaches to maintain the "virtual team" relationship with the other informatics leaders. The first of these was co-location. The offices of the informatics leaders were in the same area, so that they encountered each other frequently. The second approach was quarterly retreats where joint plans were created and progress was reviewed. Finally, weekly "huddles" were held each Friday at a local diner where new issues were addressed. Each week numerous issues were quickly resolved through the close relationships fostered in these huddles. In other organizations, they would have grown into significant problems.

A budget that helped support some of these activities and the shared staffing was critical to success. It wasn't large, but it helped.

Build on the Strengths of Your Virtual Team(s)

Getting the right people is important, but even Dream Teams may fail if they don't capitalize on each other's strengths and shore up their weaknesses. Some people are good at organizing. Others are good at communicating. Finding the team's strengths is a key task for the CMIO. Capitalizing on these strengths to achieve goals and objectives is not easy, but it is critical.

Alternately, weaknesses of informatics team leaders can be detrimental to a CMIO's success. Being aware of the team's weaknesses is important. Designing a plan to help your informatics leaders reduce their weaknesses—whether they report to you or not—can be the difference between success and failure for a CMIO.

Building successful "virtual teams" also requires identifying and developing future leaders. CMIOs should work with their "virtual team" towards creating a common informatics orientation program for new leaders and support informatics training as much as possible.

Do Informatics Titles Matter?

Informatics work is happening in organizations every day by people who don't have formal titles like "CNIO." So are titles really important?

Perhaps in a perfect or very small organization they aren't, but few of us work in these sorts of places. Wherever there are departments that require leaders, titles form an important part of how we communicate relationships. Informatics titles are particularly important in larger organizations so that the various clinical informatics leaders are properly respected at executive team levels.

In the Case Study, the CMIO permitted only one other "Chief" position because of the confusion that multiple "Chief" titles can cause. But the CMIO used "CNIO" deliberately to help the organization understand the importance of the CNIO role. The culture and structure of the organization will guide the CMIO in what titles are needed.

It is very important in the CMIO's "virtual team" that people leave their titles "parked at the door." Each discipline deserves respect and it does not help teamwork if the team members pull rank.

In cases where an informatics role is filled by a physician, the title of "Medical Director of [Clinical Area] Informatics" (e.g., Medical Director of Transplant Informatics) often carries enough weight to gain the respect and support that is needed by the CMIO and the individual with the title.

Reporting Relationships: Centralized or Decentralized?

Whether the CMIO's team should be a central department reporting to the CMIO or whether its members should be reporting into operations departments depends upon the organization's maturity, culture, and the leadership strength of the CMIO.

Centralized informatics groups reporting to the CMIO may be more efficient and effective because less energy needs to be devoted to aligning goals and expectations. But there can be an administrative cost to such an approach in terms of the human resources work required of the CMIO and there may be a cost of having to continually manage the relationships with the operating departments without directly-reporting informatics representation in them.

Decentralized informatics reporting, where the various informatics leaders are part of their operating departments, can have the opposite efficiencies. While more energy may be required to align goals and expectations and maintain team cohesion, the time needed for human resources administrative work is reduced with fewer employees. CMIOs may also find that operational departments may be more responsive when the informatics leaders are a part of those departments, as long as there is a smoothly functioning "virtual team."

Both centralized and decentralized structures work. In the Case Study, the CMIO used the best features of each, utilizing a centralized approach to build nursing informatics capacity where one did not exist and a decentralized approach in other areas that had a better capacity to handle their direct informatics reports.

Other Key Relationships

In a large organization, the most important relationships are those of the CMIO with the operational leaders such as the CMO, CNO, COO, and others. The successful CMIO should carefully cultivate their relationship with the organization's senior leaders. Whether the informatics organization is centralized or decentralized, the CMIO needs to be seen by the executive leadership as the overall leader of the organization's informatics efforts. Note that in larger organizations this role may be played by a Chief Health Information Officer or Chief Clinical Information Officer. No matter who is the ultimate leader, it is critical that the executive suite hears a consistent message regarding informatics.

In large organizations, having individual informatics relationships in larger clinical departments is important.

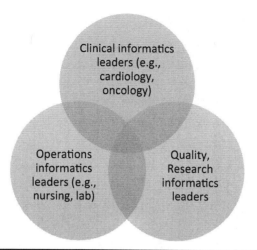

Figure 6.1 Sample informatics virtual teams.

As departments like cardiology, radiology, oncology, and others make their plans, it's important for the CMIO to be involved in these as soon as possible. Where possible, this can be done by expanding the "virtual team" concept as shown in Figure 6.1. The multiple "virtual teams" that arise from this approach can supply deep support for informatics with the CMIO's core "virtual team" consisting of key members of each circle/"virtual team."

While all clinical informatics leaders cannot be a part of the CMIO's core "virtual team," the CMIO can use the "virtual team" concept flexibly to include individual departments as needed. For example, the CMIO may have a core leadership group of five or six, including the CNIO, but may also have a larger "virtual team" that includes the clinical departments.

Develop a Shared Strategy with Your CNIO and Other Informatics Leaders

In the Case Study, the CMIO held quarterly retreats where joint plans were created and progress was reviewed. These are incredibly important because if they provide everyone with the same playbook. The CMIO and CNIO, in particular, must have a shared vision of strategy, governance, priorities, tactics, etc. and they should share in the communication of this to the CMO and CNO. Having a shared focus on quality—i.e., care that is Safe, Timely, Efficient, Effective, Equitable, and Patient-Centered (STEEEP)—can provide a common goal for the CMIO and CNIO to use as a compass.

Not all plans arise from quarterly retreats, as "things happen." In the Case Study, the CMIO used the weekly huddle to establish plans for handling such things as safety issues that might arise or other problems. Whether the huddle approach is used or not, frequent verbal and in person communication is key. Electronic communications may be necessary, but they generally do not create the interpersonal bonds that are needed for the CMIO, CNIO, and others to be successful.

The Importance of a Multidisciplinary Systems Approach

Informatics is increasingly multidisciplinary. Order sets, for example, can be developed by physicians, but nurses, pharmacists and other clinicians carry out the bulk of the orders; their participation in order to set development and governance is critical. Even development of physician documentation has an impact outside of the physician world, as it may require data elements that are captured by nurses and others, thus impacting their workflow.

A multidisciplinary systems approach also is important in determining what projects are prioritized. If the bulk of the Information Systems Department time is spent on improving physician workflow, that might be seen as a win for physicians, but in fact it can be a net loss.

In order to foster a team spirit in informatics, multidisciplinary initiatives should be promoted as "we're doing this for the patients" rather than "It's for the nurses" or "it's for the physicians." This builds multidisciplinary support and keeps the focus where it belongs. Of course, each initiative has different benefits, but the marketing of those benefits needs to be a careful balance between ensuring that each discipline understands that they are getting attention, and that no discipline feels short-changed.

Budgets

In the Case Study, the CMIO had a budget that he used to support his initiatives. Wherever possible, a budget under the control of the CMIO should be obtained. This provides flexibility and control. Shared budgets, particularly those controlled by the CIO or the CMO, should be avoided because the CMIO generally loses control over spending in these situations.

Clinical Support of End Users

The Case Study did not mention one of the more challenging interactions of the CMIO and CNIO, which is determining how end users will be supported. Nursing workflow and physician workflow are dramatically different, so it often is very difficult to train one person to do both. However, in smaller organizations this may be necessary.

If a single support team is used, it is important to make sure that they provide adequate support to all of the disciplines they cover. It is also important to ensure that their manager or team leader understands they are the public face of the CMIO and CNIO. So no matter where they report in the organization, a close relationship with the CMIO and CNIO is needed.

If the CMIO has a support group for physicians and the CNIO has a support group for nurses and other clinical disciplines, the coordination needs to happen at the CMIO/ CNIO level. This can be challenging for the relationship. Frequent verbal and in person communication is necessary.

Aligning with Research, Quality, Data Governance, Reporting, and Analytics

There are a multitude of other relationships that the CMIO must balance. Applying the "virtual team" concept similar to Figure 6.1 is an approach that has been successful.

Summary

The CMIO position in many ways is all about relationships. In this chapter, we have tried to show some of the ways that CMIOs can create "virtual teams" to build and maintain these relationships with their CNIO and other informatics leaders.

The "Healthy Vital Signs" of a successful CMIO include getting the right people identified, empowering them, and developing shared goals and objectives. Frequent verbal and in person communication with "virtual team" members and senior executive leadership is vital to the CMIO's success.

Chapter 7

Configuration, Workflow, and Document Standards

R. Dirk Stanley

Contents

If you've ever heard someone say, *The system doesn't do what it's supposed to do!*, what they're really trying to say in "Informatics speak" is, *The workflows and the configuration aren't aligned!*

This means that only *half* of the challenge of a successful Electronic Medical Record (EMR) implementation comes from your **configuration**—The other half comes from the **workflows** that drive the organization.

As a CMIO working to support that EMR, you will want to concern yourself with not only your EMR configuration, but how well it supports the many financial and clinical workflows of your organization. Sometimes problems arise from *configuration*, and sometimes they arise from *workflows*.

In the role of CMIO, you will need to understand how to document, analyze, and change **workflows**.

The problem is that **workflows** are sometimes a bit like *carbon monoxide*—They are *invisible, odorless, and tasteless*, but if you're not aware of them or how to test them, *they can hurt you*.

So what exactly is **workflow**? It helps to start with a basic definition to build upon. Definitions of **workflow** may vary, but one of the best comes from workflow expert **Charles Webster, MD** (no known relation to *Webster's Dictionary*) who describes it as:

> "...a series of tasks, consuming resources, achieving goals."[1]

I sometimes share my own variation on this:

> "Workflow is the set of ordered tasks that uses people, resources, and time to accomplish a desired goal."

Whatever definition you use, it's how the people in your organization perform their routine functions, both large and small, to organize their day, deliver care, and document that care. Think of it as the *recipe you use to get something done*.

To ensure that your EMR is well configured, you and your Informatics team will often ask:

1. What is the current workflow?
2. What is the expected workflow?
3. How well does the EMR configuration support that workflow?

This means that in an *ideal* state, you would want both workflow and configuration to be **optimal** and **perfectly aligned**, like in this visual diagram below (Figure 7.1):

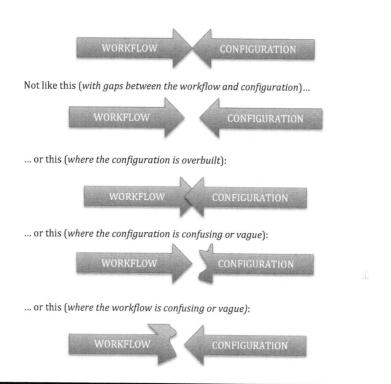

Figure 7.1   Workflow and configuration alignment.

Workflow should always drive configuration. To help make sure your workflow and configuration are both *well designed* and *well aligned,* you will first need to start with **well-defined** workflows that you can use to analyze and build your configuration.

Where do workflows come from? It's a common misconception that they come from a Visio diagram on a shared drive, or a policy/procedure in your policy manual. While those are both key tools in understanding and documenting workflows, they really arise from **all of the documents** in your organization.

This brings us to some discussion about **documents.** Documents are tools that collect, store, and transmit information. They are the lifeblood of any organization, and *all of them together* guide and shape the **workflows** of your organization. Think of them as the *DNA that makes your organization work.*

So Visio diagrams and policies/procedures are simply **summaries** of the *collective work* being done by the **people** in your organization interacting with these many **documents and tools**.

We can grossly simplify this relationship between **documents** and **employees**, to create predictable **workflows**, with the following illustration:

Generally speaking, **employees** create the ***documents (and other tools)*** that help the organization run—and if those ***documents and other tools*** are well-designed and easy-to-find, the **employees** will *read them* and *use them* to create predictable behaviors, workflows, and outcomes. *It's an informational feedback loop that goes back to our earliest human ancestors* (Figure 7.2).

So when we refer to documents and other tools, what *exactly* are we talking about?

Hint: It's much more than just an email, guideline, policy, or order set. **Workflow** is shaped by ***all*** the documents and

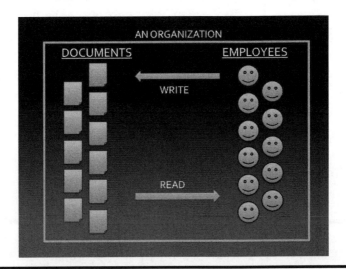

Figure 7.2 Summary of the relationship between employees and their documents.

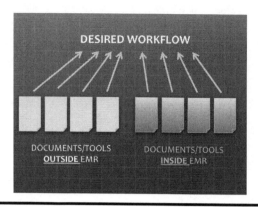

Figure 7.3 Summary of how tools both inside and outside the EMR support workflows.

tools we use in healthcare, both ***inside*** and ***outside*** of your EMR (Figure 7.3):

What *exactly* are these documents and tools, found inside and outside of EMRs which are commonly used in healthcare? You're probably already familiar with most, if not all of them (Table 7.1):

Table 7.1 Some Common Documents and Tools that Work Together to Create Your Workflows

Common Documents/Tools that Work Together to Support Workflows	
Typically Outside of EMR	*Typically Inside of EMR*
1. Plans (*Project, Testing, Education, Go-Live, etc.*) 2. Policies/procedures 3. Guidelines 4. Protocols 5. Patient consents 6. Interfaces 7. Staff/patient education modules 8. Staff schedules 9. Committee charters 10. Organization charts 11. Budgets 12. Job descriptions	1. Clinical documentation (*Notes, checklists, flowsheets, images/media, etc.*) 2. Lab/pathology results 3. Radiology images and results 4. Orders 5. Order sets 6. Clinical pathways 7. Medical logic modules (*MLMs*) 8. Best practice alerts (*BPAs*) 9. Infobuttons 10. Security groups 11. User profiles/filters 12. Reports/dashboards

While it may not be immediately intuitive, it's a common mistake to only worry about the tools *inside* the EMR. The tools *outside* have *just as much impact on workflow,* and so a CMIO has to take on the challenge of aligning **all of these tools** (*from both* inside *and* outside *the EMR*) to good, solid, evidence-based clinical workflows.

While "EMR configuration" only refers to those tools *inside* the EMR, it's important to remember that some of your configuration challenges come from *outside* the EMR. How well you align these documents/tools with your workflows will depend largely on:

1. How well you document *your current state* workflows (*point A*)
2. How well you document/design your future state workflows (*point B*)
3. How well you plan for the time, people, and resources necessary to get from point A to point B

For your team to accomplish all this in a clear, efficient manner, you will need to plan for the many meetings and hours studying the **documents and tools** that your stakeholders are *currently* interacting with, and then plan for the ones they will interact with in the *future.*

When your team assembles to discuss workflows, you may notice that at times different team members have different understandings of the functions of these documents/tools. You can spot these discrepancies at meetings, when **questions come up** about the exact function of a particular document/tool, and the regulations related to it (Figure 7.4).

When that happens, it's helpful to have solid document *definitions, templates, development processes,* and the governance necessary to develop, review, publish, and implement them effectively.

The basic guidance below shows how you can become a *gourmet workflow chef* by following some simple steps for

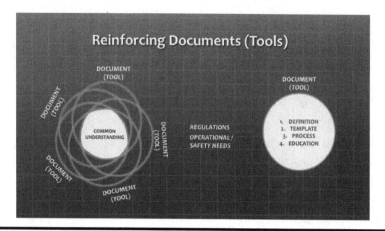

Figure 7.4 **How to turn ambiguity into concrete understanding.**

developing ("*baking*") the documents or tools necessary to support your desired ("*gourmet*") workflow:

General Nine-Step recipe for creating gourmet workflows:

1. **Conception**—Who conceives of the need for a workflow change, and when? What evidence or regulations support the need for the change?
2. **Planning**
   a. Who will study and document the current-state workflow, and the documents/tools that currently support it?
   b. Who will design and plan the future-state workflow, and the documents/tools that will be needed to support it?
   c. What is the scope of the future-state workflow? What stakeholders will be impacted?
   d. After the scope of work has been defined, who reviews the cost and approves the project *before* construction gets underway?
   e. Who plans for the development and integration of the necessary documents/tools?
3. **Drafting/Building**—Who will draft and build the future-state document(s)/tool(s) needed for your future-state workflow? Using which templates and style guides?

4. **Testing/"Vetting"**—Who will test the documents/tools?
   Using what testing plan(s)?
   a. **Unit Testing**—*Does each document/tool work by itself?*
   b. **Functional Testing**—*Do the documents/tools work in conjunction with other documents/tools?*
   c. **End-User Acceptance Testing**—*Do the end-users feel the workflow (collective documents/tools) will work and support them at go-live?*
   d. **Integration Testing**—*Will the workflow (documents/ tools) function when combined with other workflows?*
5. **Approval**—Who will approve the documents/tools, before they go live, and how?
6. **Education**
   a. Who will educate the primary and secondary stakeholders on the new workflow and the use of the documents/tools they will interact with?
   b. How and when will this education be delivered?
7. **Publication/"Go-Live"**
   a. Who will help implement or publish the documents/ tools?
   b. Where will they publish it, so the end users can access them?
   c. Who will help reinforce the education and support needed for the documents/tools to be successfully implemented?
8. **Adoption**—Who will help reinforce the education and support the end-users to successfully adopt the new workflow, and the documents/tools that support it?
9. **Monitoring/Optimization**—Who will monitor the effectiveness of the documents/tools, and how? And who will continue to correct any issues that arise?

These nine simple steps can be applied to almost *any* document, tool, or workflow development, from *policies/ procedures*, to *orders*, to *order sets*, to *guidelines*, to *staff or patient education*, and more. Using a standard development process will help you plan, and help you make sure you don't miss any important steps. If you've ever heard someone say, *Why don't the docs use this order set?* or *Why don't the staff read this policy?*, it can be a sign that of one or more of those nine steps were missed during its development and adoption.

For example, if you are developing a workflow that depends on **five tools** to function correctly, then you will want to plan for **all five tools** to *cross the finish line* together at your go-live date, and then work backwards and plan accordingly.

Having shared some tricks for gourmet-style workflow, document, and tool development, here are a few final take-home thoughts:

1. The quality of your **EMR configuration** will depend, *at least in part*, on your ability to **plan for the change** from your current-state to your future-state workflows.
2. Your ability to **plan for the change** from your current-state to future-state workflows will depend, *at least in part*, on the **quality of your current-and-future-state workflows**.
3. The **quality of your current-and-future-state workflows** will depend, *at least in part*, on the quality of the **documents and tools** you use to build and support them.
4. The quality of your **documents and tools** will depend on:
   a. Your definitions, templates, style guides, development processes, and governance (to create standards)
   b. The process by which you plan to build, test, approve, educate, and implement them

I hope this has been a helpful summary on the workflow planning, change management, and tool/document development that go into the implementation of an EMR. As you continue your CMIO journey, remember that success often depends on the tiniest details, and on building the tools, processes, and governance needed to keep projects on time and users happy with the results.

Reference

1. Webster, C. (June 13, 2014) *BPM-based Population Health Management & Care Coordination: Workflow, Usability, Safety & Interoperability Perspectives* [Web log post]. Retrieved from September 30, 2017. http://wareflo.com/2014/06/bpm-based-population-health-management-care-coordination-workflow-usability-safety-interoperability-perspectives/

Chapter 8

Personal Health Records and Health Record Banks

Richard Gibson

Contents

Introduction

Personal health records (PHRs) were first mentioned in 1978.[1]
Peter Szolovits coined the term "Guardian Angel" in 1994 to
describe an information system centered on the individual
instead of the provider.[2] The system would automatically
collect health information about the individual, interact with
the individual as needed, warn the person of necessary
actions, personalize recommendations for care, maintain
patient preferences, and educate the patient. Many people
have written about personal health information management
systems including Marion Ball,[3] Paul Tang,[4] and the Markle
Foundation. Probably the most famous examples of personal
health records are Microsoft Health Vault (established in 2007)
and Google Health (2008–2012).

The early PHRs required the consumer to do all the work
of collecting, journaling, and entering the data. For example,
patients had to type in their laboratory results. In addition to
being a lot of work for consumers, the idea never took off
with providers. The PHRs did not contain data of sufficient
importance to warrant providers taking a look. Providers did
not have enough trust of the information found in the early
PHRs because most of the data were self-reported by the
patient (this issue is addressed below).

In modern PHRs and health record banks (HRBs), most
of the data come directly from EHRs used by healthcare
providers (doctors, hospitals, labs, and diagnostic imaging
centers) and the data are copies of consumers' professional
health records and diagnostic images in those facilities. The
term "health record bank" was used to draw the analogy of

a trusted intermediary taking "deposits" of health data from providers for the benefit of a consumer, and then sending those data to another provider as requested by the consumer, similar to a consumer writing a check requesting the bank to pay someone.

PHRs and HRBs can also accept claims data from your health insurance company. PHRs and HRBs are ideal for data collected from your personal devices (fitness trackers, weight scales, glucose meters, sleep trackers, etc.) and self-reported data via mobile phone apps (nutritional diaries, symptom trackers, etc.). Both PHRs and HRBs can store and display data entered directly by the consumer. Both PHRs and HRBs are managed by the consumer or an agent of the consumer (as opposed to EHRs, which are managed by providers). For the rest of this note, the term "PHR" will be used synonymously with "HRB."

Personal Health Records and Patient Portals

Most health systems have EHRs and most ambulatory providers have office electronic medical records (EMRs). Most EHRs and EMRs have connected patient portals for consumers to be able to see lab results, schedule appointments, request refills, and communicate with their providers—all valuable functions. But patients who don't get all of their care at just one health system have to remember logins, passwords, and navigation tools for multiple patient portals, which tends to diminish the use of patient portals in general. When patients see a new provider, the portals are not helpful to inform the new provider about the patient's prior care. And when the consumer's insurance company changes or they move geographically, they have to pick up with new providers and all their previous data are locked in prior EMRs and portals.

Personal Health Records and Health Information Exchange

Health information exchange involves providers sending patient data among themselves in a many-to-many scattered distribution, just in time to prepare the next consultant to see the patient. If records are not sent in advance of a visit, the provider needs to go out and request record transfer from multiple prior providers. Then the provider needs to assimilate and organize all the incoming data on the fly while seeing the patient.

With a PHR, the patient's account receives a deposit after every visit from every provider they see in a many-to-one model. Sophisticated PHRs can organize the multiple streams of incoming data, eliminate duplicate data, highlight conflicting data, and prepare a single organized view of the data for the next provider to view at the time that they see the patient.

Personal Health Records and Health Information Exchanges (HIEs)

In the relatively few regions that have effective health information exchanges (HIEs), each provider sends a copy to the HIE of new data added to their EMR after a visit, including new problems, medications, allergies, vital signs, lab results, and so forth. If the patient sees a new provider, presumably they can log into the HIE and see data detailing much of the prior care of the patient. When HIEs work, they are helpful in delivering information to the point of care. But PHRs can improve upon HIEs in the following ways:

■ Some HIEs do not maintain a persistent record, they only exchange data. PHRs are a permanent repository.

- If a patient changes his or her name, it could be a problem for HIEs. PHRs are immune to this problem.
- HIEs require broad governance among many stakeholders. PHRs require only a repository trusted by the consumer.
- HIEs are correctly perceived as the Providers' Record. Some of the most successful HIEs in the country don't even have a patient-facing application. PHRs are the Consumer's Copy of the Professional Record.
- Most HIEs don't handle diagnostic imaging and genomic data. Most PHRs are able to manage these data, and collect them all in one place. Increasingly, the sheer volume of these data will require that they be stored in just one place where all providers can access them when needed.
- HIEs are not very helpful when the patient moves geographically. PHRs follow the patient and can be accessed anywhere in the world the patient might travel.
- HIEs don't allow consumers to run apps against their data. Increasingly, PHRs will provide this platform.
- If there is an error in the data, patients have to go back to all their providers and correct the error. With a PHR, the consumer corrects the error in one place and all future providers see the corrected data.
- It is difficult for the consumer to control who sees their data in an HIE. Controlling access to data in a PHR is the very essence of a personal health record.
- HIEs generally don't accept the consumer's personal device data. PHRs are an ideal platform to store patient generated health data and make those data available for viewing by all of the consumer's providers.

It is too early to assess the cost of building and maintaining health record banks at scale. Multiple different PHR business models exist, which can lead to wide variation in the cost of the PHR passed on to the consumer.

PHR Purchasers and the Various Purposes Behind PHRs

Many of the PHRs have a direct-to-consumer channel. Other PHRs display a record to the consumer as a side benefit of data collected for some other purpose, such as the following:

- Collecting consumers' healthcare data to qualify them for life insurance
- Building a care coordination platform for provider groups, payers, and ACOs and the collected clinical data are displayed to consumers
- Constructing a portal for diagnostic image management companies
- Managing data exchange among providers, payers, life insurance companies, self-insured employers, and HIT vendors, and offering PHRs directly to consumers
- Offering an independent patient portal for physicians who don't wish to use or don't have access to a patient portal provided by their EMR vendor
- Supporting clinical trials for phamaceutical firms and collecting disease-specific data from patients via surveys

There is enormous value in unified, comprehensive, lifetime electronic health records. PHRs serving the above purposes can derive sufficient income from other uses of the data, allowing the PHR to be offered at no charge to the consumer. When PHRs are used at scale, medical and pharmaceutical companies will likely pay consumers and patients for access to their de-identified and identified data. Clinical trials always struggle to identify qualified study candidates and they need more data to track trial participants. Pharmaceutical vendors and medical device firms continually seek more "real-world data" to provide postmarket surveillance of products.

Consumer Account Registration

Some of the PHR firms register the consumer simply by consumer demographic information and consumer login and password. The firms then use this information to request EMR data on the patient's behalf.

Some PHR firms use a Direct address for the firm's general inbox but then parse the incoming data into the individual user accounts. Most firms that deal in Direct give each consumer their own Direct address. There are at least three levels of rigor as applied to proving the identity of the consumer: NIST (National Institute of Standards and Technology) Level of Assurance 1 (LoA1), LoA3, and Federal Bridge Medium Level.[5] LoA1 is essentially consumer login and password, as Microsoft Health Vault had.

LoA3 firms require some combination of the following in order to issue a consumer Direct address:

- Demographic information
- Valid driver's license
- Valid credit card
- An email address that the consumer can use to respond to a message
- A mobile phone with texting that the consumer can use to respond to a message
- A postal mail address that the consumer can use to respond to a message
- Knowledge-based questioning where the consumer identifies general numbers, accounts, and addresses that they have used in the past (like the method that U.S. credit agencies use to establish one's identity when one requests one's annual credit report online)

LoA3 Direct addresses can be purchased online for $10 in about 10 minutes or less. These LoA3 addresses come with X.509 certificates that are part of the DirectTrust trust network.

The provider can be assured that the patient is who he or she says he or she is. Providers and patients belonging to that trust network can send to and receive from each other without difficulty. Some ONC-certified EHRs may not send to or receive from LoA1 Direct addresses because of lack of assurance about the consumer's identity.

Federal Bridge Medium Level Direct addresses have a few more organizational and technical requirements than LoA3. This level is required to send and receive healthcare to and from any of the branches of the Federal government like the Veterans Administration, the Indian Health Service, Centers for Medicare and Medicaid Services, etc. The identity proofing is similar to that noted above for LoA3.

In addition to identity-proofing the consumer at the point of account creation, a number of PHR firms require two-factor authentication for each subsequent login to the PHR to be sure that the consumer is still the same individual as the person who created the account.

Where Do the Data Come From?

The original PHRs, like Microsoft Health Vault and Google Health, required the consumer to enter most of the data about their prior health history. There is still a place for consumer self-entry but enormous value can come from collecting data from the office EMRs of providers that the patient has seen. The ideal to keep in mind is that once the consumer has requested their provider to send them a copy of their data, that office will continue to update the PHR whenever new entries are made to the EMR, until such point as the consumer revokes the request. Most of the effort to establish PHRs is at the beginning, when consumers need to recall all the offices where they have been seen so that data can be requested.

Transfer of Data from the EMR to the PHR

Figure 8.1 shows the various ways that PHRs collect professional EMR data. All the PHR firms see FHIR as the future although very little data now comes to PHRs via that route.

Most of the PHR companies ask the consumer what providers they have seen in the past. Some firms have the consumer choose providers from a list the company provides. Other firms ask the consumer to type in the full names and addresses of providers and the company tries to correlate those entries with a list of all providers they possess. Once the PHR company knows the providers to reach out to, they send a fax or an email message requesting that the provider upload the patient's EMR data to a secure website. Many PHR companies send a Direct protocol message to the provider and request the patient's data to be returned via a Direct message. At this time, responding to a Direct request still requires a human to be involved.

Some other PHR companies ask the consumer to enter their login and password for the patient portal for each provider where they have set up a portal account. Then the company goes to the patient portal sites, collects the data, and imports it into the PHR.

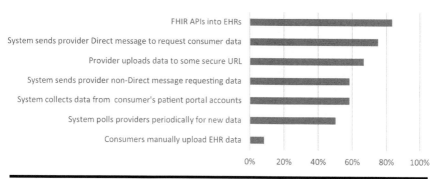

Figure 8.1   **Methods for Collecting Data into PHR.**

One PHR company receives a lot of EHR data via faxed documents. They then apply optical character recognition, natural language processing, machine learning, and finish with a human review of the record. Their record tends to have many more text documents (operative notes, consultation notes, diagnostic imaging interpretations, pathology notes, and so forth) than the other PHR companies.

One company is unique among the PHR companies surveyed in that it acts as a node on the CommonWell network and therefore has access to a wide range of documents, even unstructured text documents, found at patients' providers who are CommonWell members.

All of the PHR firms store health record data in the cloud or in similar private data centers where the consumer is able to access the record from PCs, laptops, tablets, and mobile phones.

FHIR and PHRs

Nearly all of the PHR companies said that they are planning on loading data into their PHRs via FHIR interfaces to EHRs, although only a few of them are doing so at present. FHIR is currently the best plan for EHR data acquisition long-term because it can be operated 24×7 without human intervention. Each EHR vendor exposes different "resources" or data fields to FHIR but over time, more and more of the EHR data should be accessible via FHIR. FHIR and Consolidated Clinical Document Architecture (C-CDA) are coming together so that the data elements called for by C-CDA can be acquired via FHIR. As with Query and Retrieve and Direct messaging, a trust agreement needs to bind all parties to the exchange. Trust frameworks and networks allow each organization to avoid serial one-to-one sharing contracts and agree to the rules of the network. Then all members can exchange data with each other with mutual accountability and without discrimination. A trust network for FHIR is needed for this method to become widespread as a PHR data source.

Format of the Health Record Transfer and Received Data

The Veterans Administration was the first large organization to involve patients in downloading their medical record data. The VA launched the Blue Button Movement, which was then moved to other organizations for continuing support. It appears that the Blue Button record transfer has largely been supplanted by C-CDA formatted messages although Blue Button continues as a rallying cry for involving consumers in their health data.

For most of the health record transfers to most of the PHR firms, the format of the data received from provider EMRs is that required for Meaningful Use Stage 2 (MU2), 2014 EHR Certification. These MU2 2014 EHR Certification documents come closest to the HL7 CCD (Continuity of Care) C-CDA document template with the addition of some section templates to cover data elements listed in the Common Clinical Data Set for MU2. Beyond the header section, only 4 of the 17 CCD section templates are required: Problems, Medications, Allergies, and Results. Consequently, most of the PHRs have a relatively thin set of data, even as they obtain CCDs from multiple providers.

Most of the PHRs say they will accept and display other document formats including HL7 messages, text, pdf, and image formats like jpg and gif, but they generally cannot parse those document types into sections that can be combined with like data from another EMR or used to make a summary document for the next provider. One PHR firm says that they collect X.12 formatted data (billing data).

Some of the PHRs claim to collect diagnostic images but most PHRs stick to the typical structured document formats above.

Data Types Accepted in the PHRs

Most the PHR companies accept EHR data and lab data, and nearly all claim to accept clinical photos, diagnostic images, image interpretation reports, and data from personal mobile devices. About half say they could handle genomic data, microbiomic data, and billing data as shown in Figure 8.2.

As far as consumer-entered data, most of the PHRs say they handle the common historical medical sections such as past medical history, past surgical history, family history, health habits and social history, medications, and allergies. Some accept symptoms and advance directives.

Personally-Entered Data vs EMR Data

Both personally-entered and professionally-captured data have value, but in different ways. One of the purposes of

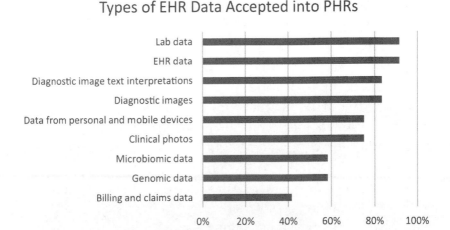

Figure 8.2   Types of EHR Data Accepted into PHRs.

PHRs is informing the consumer's next provider, especially a provider never seen before. A single, complete, de-duplicated, reconciled, lifetime record would be very helpful to a new primary care provider meeting the patient for the first time. Ideally, the PHR would have the provider view organized in the format expected by most providers, with sections for problem list, past medical history, surgical history, family history, health habits and social history, medications, allergies, and so forth. Most current PHRs are not yet sophisticated enough to reconcile complex data feeds from multiple EMRs into a single, clean list. But over time, this functionality is likely to improve.

If a provider is going to use the PHR to inform their care, they will need to trust that the data they are seeing in the PHR has not been edited or tampered with by the consumer. Documents sent by other providers' EMRs can be delivered with encryption and certificates guaranteeing that they have been received intact. All EMRs suffer from being incomplete, not by any misuse by the provider but because it is hard and time-consuming to collect all of the historical data that might be valuable to a given provider or another provider at some future time. Of course, all "subjective" data, those data elements told by the patient during the provider's interview, are likely to be different in specifics and in completeness each time the patient tells his or her story. Providers work hard to capture useful information but the process is imperfect at best. If a patient has been with a provider a long time, there is a better chance that the EMR record will be relatively complete.

If problems from the problem lists of multiple EMRs are combined, for example, into a comprehensive PHR problem list, the tamper-proof guarantee of a given provider's EMR summary document is necessarily broken for that display. Therefore, PHRs may have to offer two presentations of the data: one displaying a sequence of tamper-proof documents from each of the patient's providers and the other showing the PHR compilation of the major sections of the patient's medical history, collated from multiple EMR sources. Sophisticated PHRs can link an entry in a collated list back to the tamper-proof document whence it came, thereby satisfying both requirements of summary data and untouched EHR documents.

Another use of PHRs is replacing the clipboard thrust into the hands of new and returning patients for them to handwrite their past history in the waiting room. This occurs even in provider offices that are fully on electronic medical records. A number of the current PHR companies allow the consumer to fill out all of the above history sections at home—once—and then forward it to each new provider they see in the future, saving consumers from hours of scribbled entries on a clipboard in the waiting room and saving providers from reentering those data into their EMR. Such data might be more useful to the provider if the history document from the patient could be automatically imported into the provider's EMR.

A valuable use of PHRs is for consumers to comment and offer corrections to data derived from provider EMRs. For example, a consumer could correct the laterality of a procedure or how an injury occurred when an error appears in the provider's data. The PHR allows the consumer to make the correction just once and all future views of the PHR by providers will display the corrected data. The patient's entry could appear side-by-side with the corresponding provider entry without breaking the tamper-proof seal of documents from provider EMRs.

Provider Access to Consumer Data in the PHR

Most HRBs allow providers to view patient data directly in the HRB (via a "provider portal") while also retaining the ability to send the data to providers' EMRs. Sending data to providers via pdf file is more common than sending via

C-CDA. A key HRBA principle is that each consumer controls access to the data in his or her account. The consumer can then add various individuals to the account and give them read-access to the account data, including providers, other care givers, family, friends, or even researchers or commercial enterprises. Additionally, consumers may want to limit the data that a given viewer can see. For example, a consumer may not want his orthopedist to see that he was treated for a sexually-transmitted infection. This is understandable. But there is a risk that providers will not rely on PHRs to inform them about the patient if providers believe that a significant part of the record has been redacted. Of particular concern is medications. Let's say for example that a patient hides from a provider that she is taking an antidepressant medication and the provider prescribes a new medication that has an interaction with the antidepressant. If the provider relied solely on the PHR to inform that office visit, and did not ask the patient about all her medications, patient injury could result. For providers to rely upon PHRs, they will need to be confident that they are seeing a complete and accurate record of care in the PHR.

PHR Data Privacy and Security Aspects

One of the key benefits of health record banks is that consumers have greater control over who sees their medical records. Most consumers want their providers to see all of their prior records but they are concerned about nonproviders having access to their data without permission.

One of the core principles of the Health Record Banking Alliance is that PHRs and HRBs decrease the risk of breach of personal data by not storing thousands or millions of records in one database accessible with the breach of just one password. HRBA recommends that each consumer's record be stored under a unique key managed by the consumer.

This database key is different from the login and password the consumer uses to open the PHR application. The concept is that no one, even a PHR company database administrator, has access to patient data without consumer consent. The consumer can make their healthcare record key available to named providers as needed during care. The survey attemped to assess this capability but evidently did not make this important concept sufficiently clear. Consumers are alarmed by the numerous healthcare data breaches they read about every year and PHRs must demonstrate why consumers should trust them.

PHR Capabilities for Secondary Use of Data

One of the valuable aspects of HRBs and PHRs is that consumers can control the use of their data. Primary use of PHR data is for care rendered to the consumer by providers. Secondary uses of PHR data include research, quality and resource management, commercial use, consumer-facing applications, and so forth. Secondary uses of PHR data are also important as potential funding mechanisms for PHRs. A consumer could receive compensation for making their data available for research, either identified or de-identified.

PHR Processing Capabilities

PHRs differ widely in their ability to process data after receiving them from provider EMRs. The most important PHR function is to make the collected data organized, clear, and useful to the next provider seeing the patient. That is accomplished at the most basic level by simply displaying the multiple documents received from provider EMRs. But to make sense of the data, the next provider would need to scan through a sequence of documents to assess the patient's prior medical history. More advanced HRBs are able to combine like sections from multiple EMRs and display them in one place. For example, some PHRs can combine the problems from multiple EMR problem lists and display one overall problem list. PHRs can eliminate duplicates in such a list, but that would require access to a computable concept ontology so that the PHR can "reason" that "diabetic kidney disease" and "diabetes mellitus with nephropathy" represent the same condition. Ultimately, one of the most valuable PHR capabilities will be the ability to advise consumers on health-related issues. Over time, PHRs will distinguish themselves on such processing capabilities.

Conclusion

There exists a nascent industry of small companies providing health record banks and personal health records ready to innovate and provide consumers with their complete health record and ultimately advice about how to optimize their health and healthcare purchasing. The biggest problem facing these companies is getting the data from health system EHRs and provider office EMRs. Many providers are unaware that they are obligated to provide the consumer with a copy of their complete electronic record if asked to do so by the consumer or an agent of the consumer. Further, most consumers aren't aware that they are entitled to a copy of their full record and don't know what to do with it even if they could get it. There has not yet been a "killer app" that would cause consumers to be interested in their healthcare data. But the convergence of data from electronic health records, genomics, microbiomics, social determinants of health, and patient devices manipulated by natural language processing, machine learning, and artificial intelligence undoubtedly will produce applications that deliver enormous value to consumers and help to decrease healthcare costs. We need to start now to create the underpinnings for a vibrant health data ecosystem.

With Direct addresses as the patient identification system, Direct messages and FHIRs' APIs (application programming interfaces) as transport standards, and with C-CDA and FHIR as syntax standards, we have national consensus on the tools. The Health Record Banking Alliance envisions a future where the consumer visits the provider's office, presents their ID card, their insurance card, and their PHR card, which, when scanned, connects the provider's EMR to the patient's unified lifetime record and directs the provider's EMR to send a copy of all the patient's data to the patient's HRB at the close of the visit. We further believe that a small stimulus to incent provider offices to ask the consumer for their PHR address is all that is needed to unleash a torrent of innovation. That stimulus might be something as simple as the provider office giving the patient a "Notice of PHR Data Availability" or requiring practice management systems to have a mandatory field for the patient's PHR address. We could follow the lead of eRx, which rewarded physicians initially using it with a 0.5% Medicare bonus, and incented physicians to send their patients' data to health record bank accounts. Finally, in order to have sufficient data to drive innovation, we need to motivate providers and EHR vendors to enable standard FHIR APIs to unlock all of the data (FHIR resources) sequestered in EHR databases and send them along to the consumer's health record bank account.

Both with high-deductible health plans and value-based care, consumers must become increasingly involved in shared clinical decision-making and seeking the best value for their healthcare dollar, whether with a mobile app, a face-to-face provider visit, or a telemedicine consultation. Health record banks and personal health records are foundational to all aspects of health and healthcare.

About the Health Record Banking Alliance

The Health Record Banking Alliance is a 501(c)(6) organization founded in 2006 and is dedicated to education and advocacy for health record banks and personal health records.

References

1. Computerisation of personal health records. *Health Visitor,* 51(6):227, 1978. PMID 248054.
2. Szolovits P, Doyle J, Long WJ et al. *Guardian Angel: Patient-Centered Health Information Systems.* Technical Report MIT/LCS/TR-604, MIT Laboratory for Computer Science, 1994.
3. Ball MJ, Smith C, Bakalar RS. Personal health records: Empowering consumers. *J Health care Inf Mgt,* 21(1):76–86, 2007.
4. Tang P, Ash J, Bates D et al. Personal health records: Definitions, benefits, and strategies for overcoming barriers to adoption. *JAMIA,* 13(2):121–126, 2006.
5. National Institute of Standards and Technology. 2017. http://nvlpubs.nist.gov/nistpubs/Legacy/SP/nistspecialpublication800-63-1.pdf. Accessed September 2017.

Chapter 9

Personal Health Records—A Practical Checklist for Implementation

Albert S. Chan

Contents

Background

Consumers of healthcare are increasingly expecting a digitally engaged world. Up to 56% of patients have sought out online advice or remote care in 2016.[1] Personal health records (PHR) offer tremendous promise for patient engagement, provider outreach, and operational efficiency. Yet, the rate of patient adoption has opportunities for improvement. According to a recent Office of the National Coordinator for Health Information Technology Data Brief, only 38% of patients were offered access to a PHR by a healthcare provider or insurer in 2014.[2]

There are a number of key factors that predict a successful PHR deployment. These factors were compiled into a checklist that can be leveraged for initial implementations or to review existing deployments for improvement opportunities. This is drawn from a 15-year experience supporting one of the earliest and largest PHR deployments in the United States.

Executive Readiness

At the heart of any successful health information technology implementation is alignment of the key stakeholders. PHR implementations represent a significant change in workflows for providers, clinical operations staff, and patients. Alignment of the entire organization starts with the executive leadership team and the board of directors. Optimally, all clinicians are required to participate in the implementation of the PHR. Organizations that allow individual clinicians to opt out undercut the shared culture required for a successful implementation and presents a confusing service delivery model to patients. It is difficult to explain to patients why certain individuals do not participate in the PHR offering.

PHR leaders should invest in fully defining the business case for the organization and articulating the true cost of implementation in advance of launch. This should include *workflow analysis*, a detailed mapping of common workflows, particularly in regard to patient communications and release of ancillary results that will likely to pose challenges during launch. Prelaunch efforts to incorporate countermeasures and directed training to overcome these challenges will facilitate a much smoother transition.

Patient Adoption

Patient adoption is essential to the realization of benefits of PHR implementations. Without significant patient adoption, patients will not have access to these features. Similarly, organizations who invest significantly with the vision of advancing patient engagement will not achieve anticipated benefits realization from the implementation. A number of strategies may be utilized to recruit patients to activate his/her patient portal account. The following is a review of strategies and the pros and cons of each strategy.

Point-of-Care Enrollment

One of the most effective methods of recruiting patients to enroll in personal health records is during a face-to-face interaction with the patient. Typically, the patient will come to the clinic for an encounter with a clinician and the subsequent workup may include some ancillary testing such laboratory or a radiology test. In anticipation of the release of these results via the patient portal, the patient is incentivized to complete the enrollment process. The workflow can be a simplified enrollment process after verification of the patient's identity. The advantage of this approach is that the organization's staff can provide any needed assistance to complete the process and confirm immediately that the enrollment process was successful. Attending to other clinical staff duties may pose a true or perceived barrier to having sufficient time to enroll the patient in this fashion.

Provision of an Access Code for Future Enrollment

One common strategy is to provide an access code to the patient that can be utilized to complete the enrollment process. These codes can be often generated quickly and handed to the patient as a printed page, with minimal impact on clinician or care team workflow. The major challenge of this workflow is there may be a significant rate of patients who fail to complete the process and organizations can spend significant time attempting to secondarily contact these patients in follow up, often with uncertain efficacy.

Online Enrollment

Online enrollment into personal health record is an important method to promote patient adoption. Patients are asked a series of questions about information designed to be uniquely known by the prospective user of the PHR. Completed asynchronously outside of the clinical environment and clinical encounter, the key advantage of this approach is the avoidance of a face-to-face verification to provision access. Typically, a third party vendor will be leveraged to perform the verification with challenge questions known to the applicant. Given the privacy and security implications of leveraging online enrollment functionality, allow for significant time to review the approach with the privacy and security professionals in your organization early in the planning process (Table 9.1).

Staff Engagement

Front office and nurse staff are key evangelists for the deployment of the PHR. As the first points of contact for

Table 9.1   Available Enrollment Approaches and the Relative Cost vs. Benefit

	Lower Cost	*Higher Cost*
Higher Impact	• Point-of-care enrollment • Online enrollment • Provider benchmarking	• Incentive based contests • Direct mail campaigns from primary care practices • Giveaways • Dedicated staff waiting to enroll patients
Lower Impact	• Provision of access codes (on an after visit summary) • Mail inserts into printed billing statements	• Follow up of unused access codes • Promotional videos on endless loop in lobbies

the patient, there is a key teachable moment before the interaction with the provider about the benefits of enrollment. Personal anecdotes are particularly powerful, depicting how an individual staff member has benefitted from PHR use. The staff can then enroll the patient after the interaction.

At the time of the initial go-live, all patients including the staff may not be aware of the benefits of the service. Early in the deployment, one recommendation is to invite internal providers and staff to be early piloteers of the experience. This will build familiarity with the service from the patient and provider perspective.

A fun way to incentivize and engage staff in the initial launch of the PHR are staff drawings for departments that enroll the most patients in a monthly period. Monthly lunches and other fun giveaways keep the opportunity to enroll patients at top of mind for the staff.

Missed Opportunity Reports

A powerful tool that provides accountability and assistance to the implementation team is the use of missed opportunity reports. These reports provide visibility to patients seen in the office that were not successfully converted to enrolled patients. Operational leaders can leverage such reports to drive adoption of the standard work of enrolling a patient during the course of a clinical encounter.

Provider Engagement

The impacts of the PHR implementation are perhaps most acutely felt by the clinicians. Providers can achieve significant efficiencies from the PHR. Communication of ancillary test results such as laboratory and radiology, for example, is more efficiently released to the PHR than completing workflows to send a letter to a patient. The equivalent workflow in the PHR is attaching a simple result note to the test result, with time-date stamp confirmation that the patient received and reviewed the information. Secure messaging facilitates electronic communications between patients and family members outside of telephone or face-to-face interactions, building therapeutic alliances between patients and clinicians.[3]

Benchmarking is a useful approach to engage providers with enrolling patients and organizational targets for this initiative. For example, providers concerned with PHR adoption may be reassured by seeing colleagues whom they clinically respect with high rates of adoption. Providers may benefit from discussing best practices with their colleagues who have high percentages of online enrollment and share workflows that are sustainable in busy clinical practices. A spirit of collaboration and competition may elevate the engagement of clinicians whose support is critical for PHR patient adoption.

Recognition of the work that providers perform to serve patients via the PHR is an important element of provider engagement. One method of recognition is providing dedicated time in a clinical schedule to address messages. Another option is to provide financial remuneration in the form of fixed payment amount or relative value units (RVUs) per patient message answered. In either recognition approach, a useful adjunct corollary expectation is to only offer remuneration if a service delivery standard has been met. As an example, one organization has agreed to pay physicians for responding to messages if answered within one business day, to deliver on a service standard and improve the communication experience with patients. To prevent gaming of the incentive, this organization has agreed only to provide support for responses to inbound messages initiated by the patient, not messages initiated by the provider.

With the rise of PHR adoption in the United States, it is increasingly recognized that secure patient messages and related PHR workflows potentially represent a significant body of work for care teams to complete. One study revealed that every 3.08 hours of office visits was associated with 3.17 hours of "desktop medicine," consisting of activities such as communicating with patients through a secure patient portal, responding to patients' online requests for prescription refills or medical advice, ordering tests, sending staff messages, and reviewing test results provided by clinicians.[4] Thus, it is critical for organizations to consider both staffing approaches and recognition of clinician work in their deployment plans.

Marketing and Communications

Marketing and communications are key partners in a PHR deployment. These professionals can help create a campaign that can address the needs of internal and external stakeholders. Creating a campaign to educate the internal members of the organization about the importance of a successful implementation, and its role in healthcare delivery of the organization are important enablers. Marketing and communications professionals can assist in drafting key messages and talking points for all members of the organization to be able to share with colleagues and—more importantly—patients and their families. External marketing campaigns assist in creating an ecosystem for a successful PHR initiative. Raising awareness in the community about the benefits of the PHR can rapidly increase the rate of adoption and speed the potential benefits realization experienced by a healthcare system, such as increased connections to patients and potential cost efficiencies from use of services such as online scheduling of appointments, online renewal of medications, and online payment of bills.

Support Strategies

A final element to consider for your PHR implementation strategy is the need for a robust support model. Many PHR deployments invest significantly in the initial implementation but fail to plan for future support needs and thus, fail to see the benefits of a robust PHR implementation. PHRs are patient facing systems and thus require a consumer centric approach to support beyond the traditional information technology help desk. These representatives are important brand ambassadors of the health system.

In the modern era of connectivity, an omnichannel approach to engaging patients is recommended. Hours of operation should include hours beyond the routine business day availability to accommodate patients and families before or after the workday. Phone support remains an easily accessible medium for patients to contact the support center. Similarly, patients seek asynchronous forms of communication such as email or social media that require timely responses and thus active monitoring of these channels. Recent addition of online chat, online remote desktop access (e.g., Bomgar), and texting as media provides a synchronous means of answering patient questions that provides more privacy for patients in work or other settings where it is inconvenient to speak orally. For the health system, our experience has shown that support desk agents can handle multiple chats simultaneously, which improves support cost efficiency. To support these agents, the organization should invest in developing protocols for service agents to leverage when engaging patients.

Internally, it is equally important to dedicate institutional resources to the continual evolution of the PHR in the organization. Ideally, this is a multidisciplinary committee of clinical and operational leaders who can monitor key evolving trends of patient engagement and digital health, incorporating these learnings into the digital ecosystem of the health system. Such a committee can help the organization maintain a "future proof" strategy for the rapidly evolving needs of patients and their families in an increasingly diverse and complex healthcare landscape.

Personal Health Record Implementation Checklist

- Executive readiness
- Patient adoption
- Staff engagement
- Provider engagement
- Marketing
- Support strategies

References

1. Rock Health. 2016. https://rockhealth.com/reports/digital-health-consumer-adoption-2016/. Accessed September 2017.
2. Trends in Consumer Access and Use of Electronic Health Information, Vaishali Patel, PhD MPH; Wesley Barker, MS; Erin Siminerio, MPH, October 2015, https://dashboard.healthit.gov/evaluations/data-briefs/trends-consumer-access-use-electronic-health-information.php

3. Tang PC, Ash JS, Bates DW, Overhage JM, Sands DZ. Personal Health Records: Definitions, Benefits, and Strategies for Overcoming Barriers to Adoption. *Journal of the American Medical Informatics Association: JAMIA*, 13(2):121–126, 2006. doi: 10.1197/jamia.M2025.
4. Tai-Seale M, Olson CW, Li J, Chan AS, Morikawa C, Durbin M, Wang W, Luft HS. Electronic Health Record Logs Indicate That Physicians Split Time Evenly Between Seeing Patients And Desktop Medicine. *Health Affairs (Millwood)*, 36(4):655–662, 2017. doi: 10.1377/hlthaff.2016.0811.

Chapter 10

Analytics and Population Health

Amy M. Sitapati and Christopher Longhurst

Contents

Introduction to the Current Healthcare Landscape Driving Analytics and Population Health Expansion

> Find the right questions. You don't invent the answers, you reveal the answers.
>
> **Jonas Salk (Sherrow, 2008)**

99

Dr. Jonas Salk believed that discovery, like the creation of the first safe and effective polio vaccine, required exploration, contemplation, and collaboration in order to best serve humanity (History of the Salk Institute, 2017). Exploration begins by defining the essential questions to be posed and then using analytics and population health to answer questions which result in discovery.

Nationally, healthcare organizations are ripe to service discovery. Institutions have adopted comprehensive, integrated electronic medical records (EMR) generating terabytes of patient data. Additionally, external sources of data are flooding the environment through progress in interoperability and value-based care delivery. Healthcare delivery organizations are working to harmonize disparate sources of information in variable format and terminology that can be incorporated into decision-making. The incorporation of new data streams from precision medicine, including genomics, to patient generated data through mobile health is also quickly approaching.

The state of much of this data is frequently of poor quality, disorganized, and unstructured. That variable quality data then feeds hundreds or thousands of reports locally that may or may not be read, timely, meaningful, reliable, and accessible. Arming the right person with the right data at the right time requires governance, prioritization, and vision. Through an integrated experience we can use data driven decision-making related to clinical care, safety, quality, and business functions. We can leverage increasing volume and types of data to improve care delivery, quality, and efficiency.

Background to Lexicons, Architecture, and Data

> Standards are the key to reuse, trust, and interoperability, leading to cost reduction and quality improvement.
>
> **Tim Benson (Benson, 2012)**

The concepts of lexicons, architecture, and data structure are fundamental to analytics and enable the creation of platforms that can coalesce, sort, and share information. Lexicons, as discrete knowledge branches offer a methodology to group common terms into a mutually understandable vocabulary. Within informatics, the understanding of these terms is important in order to translate and interpret errors that are terminology related. The types of lexicons varies by information type as detailed in Table 10.1 (Sitapati et al., 2017).

Architecture is the core backbone to a good information system, and is likely to transform on a regular basis to help support the growth of the organization and complexity of

Table 10.1   Standard Lexicons Used in Clinical Informatics

Information Type	Standard	Considerations
Laboratory	LOINC	While mature labs have standardization, not all clinical lab tests encode LOINC codes
Medication	RxNorm, NDC	Clinical medications use these codes but the mapping may not be clean
Diagnosis	ICD 9, ICD 10, SNOMED-CT	Many organizations adopt ICD codes linked to problem lists and encounters however the accuracy is subject to the inherent terms and individual completing the term assignment
Radiology	RadLex, SNOMED-CT, DICOM	Standards to describe the findings and metadata related to radiologic studies exist but may be unstructured in the note
Pathology	SNOMED-CT	Standards to describe the findings and metadata related to pathologic findings but may be unstructured in the note

the systems. The architecture is built and evolves to serve the functional needs of the organization. For example, data architecture can impact where and how a specific piece of information, like a risk score, is stored relative to a collection of information, such as multiple chronic conditions. Additionally, the relative structure of the architecture can then impact the speed of retrieval and processing across large data sets. Having a working knowledge of how the data is constructed simplifies trouble-shooting problems and enhances system resiliency.

Analytics

> In God we trust. All others must bring data.
>
> **W. Edwards Deming (Finger and Dutta, 2014)**

Three big shifts in mindsets have influenced the world of data and analytics in the digital age: interlinking of data, embraced lack of precision, and respect for correlation (Mayer-Schonberger and Cukier, 2013). The basic approach to analytics includes consideration of how to enable efficiency, reuse, and self-service. The analytics should also be auditable, serve as a reliable source of truth, and be presented in such a way that it promotes shared knowledge. Internal data sources such as electronic health record data are increasingly being combined with complex external data sources including claims, mobile health, pharmacy, and other care provider information. The roadblocks in external data integration from external electronic health records are now predominately related to cost, culture, skill, and ownership. Data sharing can become a reality once there is trust, access, skill, and permission to extract and integrate data. Nevertheless, this process takes both manpower, software, hardware, and time at significant costs. Creating a shared data warehouse affords opportunity in terms of consolidated efforts but poses new challenges related to data harmonization, safety, and security.

Data validation, integrity, and governance are vital to a successful analytics program. Metadata enables good data management so that coordination and communication related to data use and repurpose is efficient and accurate. Systems for data management help to collate important value sets. Strong analytics teams need audit reports and quality reports that detail their analytics performance. By creating clear and transparent views of data quality, end users can access the data with a sense of reliability. Real-time access to dashboards and ad hoc queries using self-service tools is poised to improve our ability to expand the capacity and reduce the cost of analytics. Business intelligence tools arm analysts, clinicians, and executives with the right information to help data driven decision-making.

Population Health

> Health care reform isn't about a nameless, faceless, "system." It's about the millions of lives at stake...
>
> **Barak Obama (2017)**

Population health can mean different things to different people but fundamentally it always includes four distinct components (1) patients, (2) clinicians, (3) care managers, and (4) analytics. These four can be used then to drive high-value population health delivery through (1) patient engagement using portals, education, and messaging, (2) clinician decision support including risk scores, consolidated information, and bulk outreach, (3) coordinated care management through integrated information that is prioritized including outreach between visits, and (4) analytics which uses dashboards, registries and reporting tools. Some institutions choose different tools to support these four workflows, while others rely on a single integrated electronic health record platform. In either approach, data must be transformed to knowledge in order to be harnessed for care delivery in more efficient, connected, and effective means.

Value-based care is incentivizing health system adoption of population health tools such as electronic health record-based registries, bulk activities, bundled payments with episode-based care, integrated enrollment and claims files, access to quality performance with patient and chart level detail, risk acuity scoring, and predictive analytics. A cornerstone of a population health program is EMR-based patient registries. Registries generally house key discrete data in the form of metrics. Metrics are comprised of value sets that define a specific objective (e.g., systolic blood pressure, adherence score, risk for hospitalization).

A complex registry architecture incorporates a tiered model such that individual metrics are housed in the highest common shared location and subregistries adopt additional detailed metrics parent. Registries need to span the continuum of care delivery and address primary, secondary, and tertiary prevention. In this model, a patient at risk for cardiovascular event, might have a cardiovascular risk score in a wellness registry as part of primary prevention. For secondary prevention, patients asymptomatic with cardiovascular disease might have outreach for a medical visit, lab test, aspirin or statin related to secondary prevention. Finally, the tertiary prevention might be targeted to the symptomatic heart failure patients who are at risk for hospitalization and readmission. Active registries house cohorts of patients and may be specific to payer types, wellness, disease, and location such as those illustrated in Figure 10.1.

Clear assignment of patient and provider, known as empanelment, is often critical for integration into routine clinical workflow. Additionally, clear priorities in terms of quality metrics need to be established. This core then serves as the root to enable specific outreach to specific patients from specific clinicians. Technology is then used to activate patients through outreach between visits to reduce

49 Active Patient Registries at the University of California San Diego, Fall 2017

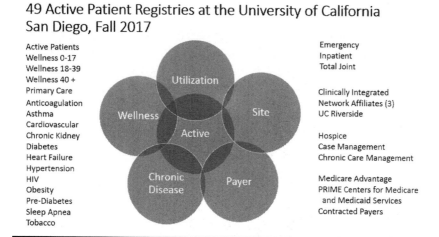

Active Patients
Wellness 0-17
Wellness 18-39
Wellness 40 +
Primary Care
Anticoagulation
Asthma
Cardiovascular
Chronic Kidney
Diabetes
Heart Failure
Hypertension
HIV
Obesity
Pre-Diabetes
Sleep Apnea
Tobacco

Emergency
Inpatient
Total Joint

Clinically Integrated
Network Affiliates (3)
UC Riverside

Hospice
Case Management
Chronic Care Management

Medicare Advantage
PRIME Centers for Medicare
and Medicaid Services
Contracted Payers

Wellness · Utilization · Site · Active · Chronic Disease · Payer

Figure 10.1   Examples of population health registry categories.

care gaps. For example, using protocols, thousands of bulk messages can accompany thousands of bulk orders specific to indicated screening mammography, lipid, and diabetic testing. Individual patients periodically need services that are provided at personalized frequency. For example, a patient with a hereditary gene for breast cancer may need alternative methods of screening and frequency. Health maintenance topics can be used to enable a personalized medicine approach to population health endeavors.

Risk acuity scoring and predictive analytics can improve patient care by identifying high-risk patients and putting them into workflows where a potential outcome or overutilization can be averted. Examples of this include cardiovascular risk assessment using the **A**rterio**S**clerotic **C**ardiovascular **D**isease (ASCVD), readmission risk assessment using **L**ength of stay, **A**cuity of admission, **C**omorbities, and **E**mergency department visits (LACE), risk of mortality for HIV patients using the **V**eterans **A**ging **C**ohort **S**tudy (VACS), and other risk acuity scores. Predictive analytics typically utilize larger data sets to forecast outcomes whether at a patient level for utilization or at an organization level to define whether particular interventions are improving care delivery.

Building systems requires close attention to the quality of the external data integration and testing. Errors in population health data can result in thousands of patients being affected. As a result, robust methods for establishing data validation and monitoring data integrity are crucial. For example, a decision to import social security death master files and convert a patient record to expired, requires a test system with production data to facilitate testing.

Approach to Leadership of Analytics and Pop Health

> The best way to find yourself is to lose yourself in the service of others.
>
> **Mahatma Gandhi (Low, 2013)**

Healthcare is undergoing significant transformation in an effort to brake the extensive accelerating costs and improve value to patients and society. As a result, the speed of landscape change requires a keen sense of current state, upcoming future state, and long-term strategic priorities. The CMIO and CIO should have a clear vision of the future, grounding for current capabilities, and sturdy enterprise-wide relationships. A key element of successful leadership is good governance.

Governance

Locally, in order to be successful in analytics and population health, healthcare organizations require leadership, governance, prioritization, and alignment. Many organizations struggle with these challenges. Creation of a solid governance process is a cornerstone to success. This governance should be owned by the operational team and inclusive of the CEO and

CFO, as well as other key organizational stakeholders that can foster alignment.

Ultimately, healthcare pivots are typically fueled by economic realities. Good leaders seek opportunities to provide analytics that help define which local goals, resources, and incentives are best poised for success (Smith et al., 2013, p271). Will your organization provide new aligned incentives to providers to help transition a path to value-based care delivery? Who will be the sponsor for this initiative? How will analytics drive the adoption? Industry standards that define how to best direct resources such as processes of continuous improvement measurement, incentives, and culture are highly valuable (Goldratt and Cox, 2004; Schein, 2004; Smith et al., 2013). Examples to this approach include the learning health system, and Lean Six Sigma that enable reassessment of goals, direction, deployment of resources, measurement of success, analysis of impact, and iterative improvement.

Longer-term strategic prioritization requires fostering interest in innovation related to technology and looking to the horizon in terms of capabilities. As new capabilities are available to improve care delivery, leadership is needed to help express how technology can support the patient, provider, community, and business needs. Use of predictive analytics and modeling, can then help the organization better gauge the optimal direction.

Future Opportunities

Biology is today an information science.

David Baltimore (Kaku, 2011)

The future is alive with urgency to transform healthcare, harness big data, and reduce health disparities. Healthcare is amidst a tsunami of revolution seeking to resolve the conflicting goals for access, quality, affordability, profit, safety, and patient-centeredness (Porter, 2010). As a result value has emerged as a guiding principle to harness improved outcomes to patients as related to incurred costs (Porter, 2010). Never have we had so many resources to spend on the lives of our patients. The U.S. healthcare budget is now 50% larger than that of the Department of Defense and plagued by high deductibles, high premiums, and high prescription pharmaceutical costs (Obama, 2017). Medicare aims to mend the fee for service reimbursement model through targeting quality improvement, utilization reduction, and growth limitation via the Medicare Access and CHIP Reauthorization Act of 2015 (MACRA) (Schneider and Hall, 2017). Vehicles such as accountable care organizations (ACOs) have been launched to promote value through patient engagement, quality improvement, and enhanced care transitions (Mostashari and Broome, 2016). This aims to enable federal influence over metrics that result in improvement in access, patient experience, outcomes, and cost.

There is an urgent need to harness "big data" in new ways to better inform the care delivery. On one hand, the published knowledge detailing therapeutic treatments and effective interventions has never been so great. An individual would have to read 2054 articles per day to digest the current output of new knowledge (Smith et al., 2013). However, we are juxtaposed with inadequate time to deliver care. The average primary care clinician with a panel of 2500 patients would need 21.7 hours per day to achieve the prevention, chronic, and acute care (Yarnall et al., 2009; Smith et al., 2013). Data in the form of public health registries, national registries, claims files, patient enrollment files, and other electronic health records, need to inform opportunities for better care. As the technology barrier is lowered, new partnerships are likely to blossom as vendors newly enter the healthcare market. The availability of integrated data will offer new opportunities for risk taking and contract diversity. Market forces may facilitate bartering of data trading that is mutually helpful. A culture of data driven decisions will increasingly be adopted not just by executive teams, but by local teams devising improvements in staffing, workflow, profitability, and access.

Historically, medicine synthesized the domains of public health, nutrition, chemistry, pharmacology, epidemiology, and scientific method (Wikipedia, 2017). In the future, we will need to fold data science and clinical informatics into the practice of medicine. Data will be used to transform the way medicine is applied and experienced. Nowhere is this likely to be more evident than in the field of genomics and personalized medicine. While insights from quantum theory fueled the explosion of genomics, the rippling effect to population health remains unchartered (Kaku, 2011). Analytics and population health will afford us the capability of transparently seeing into the future. If applied strategically, not only will we impact the lives of our individual patients, we will have the tools to help us address global health disparities.

References

T. Benson. *Principles of Health Interoperability HL7 and SNOMED.* 2nd Edition. Springer-Verlag, London. (2012).

L. Finger and S. Dutta. *Ask, Measure, Learn (Quote of W. Edwards Deming).* O'Reilley Media, Inc., Sebastopol. (2014):212.

E. M. Goldratt and J. Cox. *The Goal: A process of Ongoing Improvement.* 3rd Edition. The North River Press, New York. (2004).

History of the Salk Institute. 2017. http://www.salk.edu/about/history-of-salk/. Accessed September 2017.

M. Kaku. *Physics of the Future.* Anchor Books, New York. (2011).

P. K. C. Low. *Leading Successfully in Asia (Quote of Mahatma Gandhi).* Springer-Verlag, Berlin Heidelberg. (2013).

V. Mayer-Schonberger and K. Cukier. *A Revolution That Big Data Will Transform How We Live, Work and Think Data.* Houghton Mifflin Harcourt, New York. (2013).

F. Mostashari and T. Broome. The opportunities and challenges of the MSSP ACO program: A report from the field. *Am J Manag Care* (2016); 22:564–8.

B. H. Obama. Repealing the ACA without a replacement—the risks to American health care. *N Engl J Med* (2017); 376:297–9.

M. E. Porter. What is value in health care? *N Engl J Med* (2010); 363:2477–81.

E. H. Schein. *Organizational Culture and Leadership*. 5th Edition. Jossey-Bass, San Francisco. (2004).

E. C. Schneider and C. J. Hall. Improve quality, control spending, maintain access—can the merit-based incentive payment system deliver? *N Engl J Med* (2017); 376:708–9.

V. Sherrow and J. Salk. *Beyond the Microscope*. Revised Edition. Chelsea House, London. (2008):108.

A. Sitapati, H. Kim, B. Berkovich, R. Marmor, S. Singh, R. El-Kareh, B. Clay and L. Ohno-Machado. Integrated precision medicine: The role of electronic health records in delivering personalized medicine. *WIREs Syst Biol Med* (2017); 9:e1378.

M. Smith, R. Saunders, L. Stuckhardt and J. Michael McGinnis, Editors; Committee on the Learning Health Care System in America; *Best Care at a Lower Cost: The Path to Continuously Learning Health Care in America*. Institute of Medicine, Washington DC. (2013); p. 18.

Wikipedia. 2017. https://en.wikipedia.org/wiki/History_of_medicine. Last modified September 14, 2017.

K. S. H. Yarnall, T. Østbye, K. M. Krause, K. I. Pollak, M. Gradison and J. L. Michener. Family physicians as team leaders: "time" to share the care. *Prev Chronic Dis* (2009); 6(2):A59. http://www.cdc.gov/pcd/issues/2009/apr/08_0023.htm.

Chapter 11

Education and Professional Development for the CMIO

William Hersh

Contents

In the early days of physician informatics leadership, there was little formal training or even career paths for the Chief Medical Information Officer (CMIO) and related positions. In recent years, however, a wealth of options have emerged, including the opportunity to achieve board certification in clinical informatics as a subspecialty of all medical specialties.[1] This chapter will describe options for education and professional development for the CMIO.

Skills and Competencies

Before discussing the options, we should step back and identify the inventory of skills and competencies that a CMIO might want to function most effectively. One detailed early analysis of four CMIOs found that leadership, communication, and consensus-building were among the skills they deemed most important for success in their work. These CMIOs desired to be part of their organizations' senior physician executive team and did not want to be seen as just "techie" doctors.[2] The CMIO position is now an important part of healthcare organizations, serving as a liaison between clinicians and IT, and as the executive informatician.[3]

In recent years, increasing numbers of CMIOs report formal training, as captured in the annual Gartner survey of CMIOs by Vi Shaffer. The type of training has shifted as well, moving from business-related degrees (e.g., MBA, MHA) to those in clinical informatics. There are also various boot camps, short courses, and other options to gain knowledge and skills.

What are the competencies for clinical informaticians, including CMIOs? The original papers in *Journal of the American Medical Informatics Association* justifying training for clinical informatics subspecialty listed a set of competencies[4] and core content,[5] which are summarized in Tables 11.1 and 11.2. Another informative set of competencies for the practice of informatics comes from the American Medical Informatics Association definition and core competencies for biomedical informatics,[6] as shown in Table 11.3.

Table 11.1   Competencies for the Clinical Informatics Subspecialty

Search and appraise the literature relevant to clinical informatics
Demonstrate fundamental programming, database design, and user interface design skills
Develop and evaluate evidence-based clinical guidelines and represent them in an actionable way
Identify changes needed in organizational processes and clinician practices to optimize health system operational effectiveness
Analyze patient care workflow and processes to identify information system features that would support improved quality, efficiency, effectiveness, and safety of clinical services
Assess user needs for a clinical information or telecommunication system or application and produce a requirements specification document
Design or develop a clinical or telecommunication application or system
Evaluate vendor proposals from the perspectives of meeting clinical needs and the costs of the proposed information solutions
Develop an implementation plan that addresses the sociotechnical components of system adoption for a clinical or telecommunication system or application
Evaluate the impact of information system implementation and use on patient care and users
Develop, analyze, and report effectively (verbally and in writing) about key informatics processes

Source: Safran C et al. *Journal of the American Medical Informatics Association*, 2009. 16:158–166.

Educational Opportunities

Education options for CMIOs are highly variable, from ad hoc activities to courses to degrees and fellowships. Most of these, with the exception of graduate courses and fellowships, provide continuing medical education (CME) credit, and a growing

Table 11.2   Core Content for the Clinical Informatics Subspecialty

1. Fundamentals
1.1. Clinical Informatics
1.2. The Health System
2. Clinical Decision Making and Care Process Improvement
2.1. Clinical Decision Support
2.2. Evidence-based Patient Care
2.3. Clinical Workflow Analysis, Process Redesign, and Quality Improvement
3. Health Information Systems
3.1. Information Technology Systems
3.2. Human Factors Engineering
3.3. Health Information Systems and Applications
3.4. Clinical Data Standards
3.5. Information Systems Lifecycle
4. Leading and Managing Change
4.1. Leadership Models, Processes, and Practices
4.2. Effective Interdisciplinary Teams
4.3. Effective Communications
4.4. Project Management
4.5. Strategic and Financial Planning for Clinical Information Systems
4.6. Change Management

Source: Gardner RM et al. *Journal of the American Medical Informatics Association*, 2009. 16:153–157.

number also provide Lifelong Learning and Self-Assessment (LLSA) credits towards American Board of Preventive Medicine (ABPM) Maintenance of Certification Part II (MOC-II) requirements for the clinical informatics subspecialty.

A number of short intensive courses are available, often called "boot camps" to reflect their nature. Such courses

Table 11.3 Core Competencies for Biomedical Informatics

Acquire professional perspective: Summarize and explain the history and values of the discipline and its relationship to related fields while demonstrating an ability to read, interpret, and critique the core literature
Analyze problems: Analyze, understand, abstract, and model a specific biomedical problem in terms of data, information and knowledge components
Produce solutions: Use the problem analysis to identify and understand the space of possible solutions and generate designs that capture essential aspects of solutions and their components
Articulate the rationale: Defend the specific solution and its advantage over competing options
Implement, evaluate, and refine: Demonstrate an ability to carry out the solution, to assess its validity, and iteratively improve its design
Innovate: Create new theories, typologies, frameworks, representations, methods, and processes to address biomedical and informatics problems
Work collaboratively: Demonstrate the ability to team effectively with partners from diverse disciplines
Disseminate and discuss: Communicate effectively to audiences in multiple disciplines in persuasive written and oral form

Source: Kulikowski CA et al. *Journal of the American Medical Informatics Association*, 2012. 19:931–938.

are offered by the Association of Medical Directors of Information Systems (AMDIS, http://cmioadvisors.com/event/cmio-survival-guide-a-crash-course-atlanta-2017/) as well as the College of Healthcare Information Management Executives (CHIME, https://chimecentral.org/cmio-leadership-academy/).

Another venue for learning is conferences. The AMDIS Physician Computer Connection Symposium (http://amdis.org/pcc-symposium/) brings together CMIOs to share knowledge and experiences. The conferences of the American Medical

Informatics Association (https://www.amia.org/) also provide learning opportunities, with the Annual Symposium covering biomedical informatics much more broadly and Clinical Informatics Conference (formerly iHealth) focused on applied clinical informatics. Another event is the annual meeting of the Healthcare Information Management Systems Society (HIMSS, http://www.himss.org/), which is both an industry showcase and a source of education, including for CMIOs.

An additional common avenue for training is individual courses. Among the best known are courses from the AMIA 10 × 10 ("ten by ten") program. This program was launched in 2005 with an express goal of training one physician and one nurse in each of the 6000 U.S. hospitals by the year 2010.[7] The original course offering was an adaptation of the online introductory graduate course at Oregon Health and Science University (OHSU), with its current topic outline shown in Table 11.4. Since then, about a dozen more specialized offerings have been made available as part of the 10 × 10 program (https://www.amia.org/education/10×10-courses).

Table 11.4   Outline of the Content for the AMIA 10 × 10 Course from Oregon Health & Science University

1. Overview of Field and Problems Motivating It
2. Biomedical Computing
3. Electronic and Personal Health Records (EHR, PHR)
4. Standards and Interoperability
5. Advancing Care With the EHR
6. Healthcare Data Analytics
7. EHR Implementation and Evaluation
8. Information Retrieval (Search)
9. Imaging Informatics and Telemedicine
10. Research Informatics

An additional single-course option is board review. Although the short course is focused on covering the content of the board exam, it does provide a concentrated introduction to clinical informatics (https://www.amia.org/clinical-informatics-board-review-course). There are also board review books by Reston[8] and Finnell and Dixon.[9]

For those wanting more than a single course, the next option has been to pursue a graduate degree. Many options have emerged over the years, from traditional campus-based experiences to online offerings. One emerging trend has been the development of so-called Graduate Certificate programs, which are usually a subset of a full master's degree. Another graduate degree option is a PhD, though this is usually pursued for those seeking research and academic careers. The AMIA website maintains a catalog of such educational programs (https://www.amia.org/education/programs-and-courses).

Another option for training is a fellowship. Traditionally, fellowships in informatics were funded by the NLM (https://www.nlm.nih.gov/ep/GrantTrainInstitute.html) or VA (https://www.va.gov/oaa/specialfellows/programs/sf_medicalinformatics.asp). Although these fellowships ostensibly aimed to trained researchers and academics, many early CMIOs also were trained from them. With the emergence of the clinical informatics subspecialty, new clinical fellowships have emerged, accredited by the Accreditation Council on Graduate Medical Education (ACGME). There are nearly 30 such fellowships now, and an up-to-date list is on the AMIA Web site (https://www.amia.org/membership/academic-forum/clinical-informatics-fellowships).

Board Certification

There are a number of questions for both the established and aspiring CMIO. Probably the most common question for both is whether to seek board certification.[1] From Shaffer's annual surveys, it has been seen that the number of CMIOs who are board-certified has been growing, hitting 77% in 2016 with another 18% planning to pursue certification. While increasing numbers of CMIOs are obtaining board certification, it is not an absolute requirement for jobs at this time. It may become a highly desired attribute of candidates in the future, but it will probably be unlikely that a physician who is highly competent in clinical informatics but not board-certified will be unable to be hired. One of the unfortunate consequences of clinical informatics being a subspecialty of all specialties is that one must have active board certification in a primary specialty. This will likely be a challenge for clinical informatics who leave behind clinical work or never practiced at all.

At the time of this writing, eligibility for the subspecialty is still obtainable through the "grandfathering" period, which runs through 2022. During this time, physicians can achieve eligibility to take the clinical informatics board exam via two pathways. The first pathway is the Practice Pathway, in which those who "practice" clinical informatics at 25% time for at least 3 years of the last 5 years (education time counts at half time of practice) can become board-eligible. Experiences that qualify by this pathway include those that involve implementation and leadership of clinical informatics systems. While academic and research activities also count, just using an EHR does not. All experiences used in this pathway are additive, so candidates can mix and match various types of work experience as well as education.

A second pathway to board eligibility during the grandfathering period are so-called "nontraditional fellowships," where nontraditional means those not accredited as clinical fellowships by the ACGME. These include the traditional fellowships described above that are funded by the NLM and VA, although some of the VA fellowship have transitioned to ACGME-accredited formats. A master's degree from institutions funded by the NLM and VA also qualifies under this pathway.

An additional pathway to become board-certified now is through the new ACGME-accredited clinical informatics fellowships. One of the challenges of all fellowships is that at this time, they all require a 2-year, on-the-ground experience. While this is probably the gold standard for clinical informatics training, it may be difficult for a mid-career physician with an established job and/or family.

The clinical informatics subspecialty is open to physicians of all primary specialties (e.g., internal medicine, family medicine, pediatrics, surgery, radiology, etc.). The administrative home for the subspecialty is the American Board of Preventive Medicine (ABPM, http://www.theabpm.org/become-certified/subspecialties/clinical-informatics) for all but pathologists, who have a separate process (although take the same board examination) through the American Board of Pathology (http://www.abpath.org/index.php/to-become-certified/requirements-for-certification?id=40). This author's interpretation of the eligibility process can be found in his blog (http://informaticsprofessor.blogspot.com/2017/07/eligibility-for-clinical-informatics.html).

Continuing Education

Does the established CMIO need education? Clearly such an individual needs to keep up to date to work effectively, understanding new technologies at least at a high level, while also being current with regard to the healthcare system and its reform, emerging trends such as value-based care and population health, and state-of-the-art management and personnel practices. It is likely that the emerging continuing medical education (CME) and maintenance of certification (MOC; required for board-certified subspecialists) will provide educational experiences even for those who are not board-certified. Those who are board-certified will need to complete the four parts

Table 11.5 Continuing Education Options for Board-Certified Clinical Informatics Subspecialists

	Recertification Year 2024–2025	*Recertification Year 2016 and beyond*
Part 1	Online attestation of valid U.S. or Canadian medical license	Online attestation of valid U.S. or Canadian medical license
Part 2	175 CME credits, including at least 70 LLSA credits 1 Patient Safety Module in years 1 or 2 of cycle	250 CME credits, including at least 100 LLSA credits 1 Patient Safety Module in years 1 or 2 of cycle
Part 3	Written exam in years 8, 9 or 10 of cycle	Written exam in years 8, 9 or 10 of cycle
Part 4	2 practice performance projects	3 practice performance projects

of MOC as outlined in Table 11.5 (https://www.theabpm.org/wp-content/themes/abpm-public-site/docs/3_CI_MOC_requirements_by_year.pdf). The ABPM Web site allows searching for clinical informatics MOC (http://moc.theabpm.org/moc/modules-llsa-moc.cfm).

The Aspiring CMIO

What about education for the aspiring CMIO? The choice for educational path is likely driven by whether or not he or she desires board certification. The uptake of board certification has been rapid, although that trajectory may change at the end of the grandfathering period. Nonetheless, it is likely that many future CMIO positions, especially in health systems, will require board certification (with those in other settings, such as industry, less likely to require it, akin to industry employment for physicians of other specialties).

After 2022, the only pathway to board certification will be an ACGME-accredited clinical informatics fellowship. For physicians not pursuing board certification, there are other educational pathways, such as graduate programs and NLM fellowships listed above.

The Future

Regardless of what happens with board certification, the modern CMIO needs to master a knowledge base and skill set to function most effectively. If nothing else, these competencies will be required to be competitive for CMIO jobs. Fortunately, there are currently many education and training options to acquire them.

References

1. Detmer DE and Shortliffe EH, Clinical informatics: Prospects for a new medical subspecialty. *Journal of the American Medical Association*, 2014. 311:2067–2068.
2. Leviss J, Kremsdorf R, Mohaideen MF, The CMIO—a new leader for health systems. *Journal of the American Medical Informatics Association*, 2006. 13:573–578.
3. Kilbridge P, *Maximizing Your CMIO's Effectiveness*. 2012, The Advisory Board Company: Washington, DC, http://www.advisory.com/Research/IT-Strategy-Council/Research-Notes/2012/Maximizing-Your-CMIOs-Effectiveness.
4. Safran C, Shabot MM, Munger BS, Holmes JH, Steen EB, Lumpkin JR et al., ACGME program requirements for fellowship education in the subspecialty of clinical informatics. *Journal of the American Medical Informatics Association*, 2009. 16:158–166.
5. Gardner RM, Overhage JM, Steen E, Munger BS, Holmes JH, Williamson JJ et al., Core content for the subspecialty of clinical informatics. *Journal of the American Medical Informatics Association*, 2009. 16:153–157.

6. Kulikowski CA, Shortliffe EH, Currie LM, Elkin PL, Hunter LE, Johnson TR et al., AMIA Board white paper: Definition of biomedical informatics and specification of core competencies for graduate education in the discipline. *Journal of the American Medical Informatics Association*, 2012. 19:931–938.
7. Hersh W and Williamson J, Educating 10,000 informaticians by 2010: The AMIA 10 × 10 program. *International Journal of Medical Informatics*, 2007. 76:377–382.
8. Reston R and Pope C, *Clinical Informatics Board Review: Pass the Exam the First Time* (3rd Edition). 2017, InformaticsPro Incorporated: San Diego, CA.
9. Finnell JT and Dixon BE, eds. *Clinical Informatics Study Guide: Text and Review*. 2016, Springer: New York, NY.

Chapter 12

The CMIO and Privacy and Security

Eric M. Liederman

Contents

Nothing threatens trust in electronic health records (EHRs), Health Information Exchanges (HIEs), and other clinical information systems like breaches in privacy and security. In 2009, a British physician, Andrew Jamieson, accessed the "Spine," the UK's HIE, to view the medical records of multiple politicians and celebrities, including the sitting Prime Minister, Gordon Brown, "out of curiosity" (Silvester 2010). The widespread publicity about this snooping breach led to an immediate and catastrophic fall in support for the Spine among physicians and the British public, precipitating its collapse. Since then, no replacement for the Spine has been proposed, let alone implemented.

In recent years, external cyberattacks on healthcare systems have escalated, adding a new and dangerous threat to that of insider snooping. In some cases, healthcare institutions have been directly targeted—by state actors, cyber criminals, and hacktivists—and in some cases have suffered collateral damage from attacks targeted elsewhere. In all cases, the result is a devaluation of trust in the electronic systems that CMIOs and their colleagues have worked so hard to install and maintain, in support of the collaborative care needed for holistic patient care.

Negative ramifications from breaches come from within and outside an organization. Externally, regulators may impose fines, require media and patient notification, and demand changes to privacy and security protocols. Patients, insurers and payers may threaten to or actually take their business elsewhere. Internal leaders, responding to these pressures, often decide to lock down access to EHRs and other systems, thereby impairing care delivery. CMIOs need to represent the interests of clinicians and patients by highlighting the negative impacts to patient care that would result from proposed privacy and security changes.

The goal of the CMIO should be to help his or her organization find an optimal balance between the aspirations of collaborative, connected patient care, and the risks of insider snooping and external cyberattacks. The definition of that balance is where the aggregate risk to patient safety and quality, and to privacy and security, is lowest. A wide-open system with no protections is just as unacceptable as is a system so locked down as to be unusable.

Balance is not easily achieved in the heat of battle; in response to a major breach, emotions run high and decisions skew in the direction of lockdown. To be effective, the CMIO must work, plan, and collaborate continuously, to create and garner support for approaches that achieve and maintain risk balance. The first step is to establish working relationships with security, compliance, and audit leaders in the organization. These dedicated professionals are not the enemy; they are charged with responsibilities to protect the organization, and both they and the CMIO will be more effective by learning each other's perspectives and goals.

The second step is to use these shared learnings and perspectives to mutually develop problem statements about the two broad categories of threats: (1) snooping by authorized users, and (2) attacks by external threat actors. These problem statements should then be used to create options, and then action plans for prospective prevention, and post hoc reaction.

Let us first examine the threat from authorized users. These individuals have been given logins for good reasons, most often for direct care delivery. What induces them to access medical records without a justifiable cause? The driver is almost always curiosity, often triggered by a temporary event, such as a hospitalization or news story. These people typically have fully functioning consciences, and first have to rationalize their actions—"I wonder if there is anything I can do to help"—to convince themselves it is ok to snoop. When confronted about their snooping, they typically feel remorse; if reminded that snooping is wrong, they will deter themselves. Rarely, the insider breach actor is a sociopath, who knows that what they are doing violates laws, norms, and rules, and doesn't care. These dangerous actors must be found and held accountable.

How to deter rationalizers and identify sociopaths? Forensic data mining and analysis—what the HIPAA Security Rule calls "System Activity Review" (SAR). Finding suspicious lookups accomplishes both aims. The existence of such a program causes most rationalizers to self-deter, and finds the sociopaths. Audit logs record who accessed the records of which patients, when, and for how long. They also contain demographic information about patients. Human Resources (HR) systems contain demographic information about system users, and about those patients who are also employees. Insurance systems contain information about who is currently—or was in the past—on the same insurance plan. Irrespective of motivation, insiders snoop on those they know personally such as family, coworkers, and friends, or who they know of—prominent leaders in the organization or community, and those in the news.

Data from these systems can be combined and analyzed to identify inappropriate record access, focusing on those relationships that drive snooping. Reports can be created manually, can be generated by vendor-provided systems, or can be produced by big data analytics engines using risk scores. However they are produced, lists of possible snoopers should have few false positives (i.e., have high specificity), so as not to wear down and demoralize the staff conducting investigations. To this end, results of investigations should be fed back to those maintaining the SAR system, to allow them to create filters and make other changes to reduce false positives.

The intent of SAR is to deter snooping, not to fire everyone. Therefore, before running the first reports, communicate widely that an enhanced monitoring program will be started on a certain date, and then a week later start running regular weekly reports, looking back a week. During resulting investigations, no such time limits apply—past behavior can and should be examined, to find serial snoopers, who may be sociopaths. Despite the communication, some will still snoop, and their being held accountable will resonate widely. Snooping can be expected to drop rapidly and dramatically—in my experience in several health systems, by over 95% in a matter of weeks.

Some relationships and individuals generate heightened temptation to snoop, which can break through the self-deterrence created by an effective SAR program. Examples include family members, internal leaders, and people in the news. A powerful adjunctive tool for such situations is a "Break the Glass" (BTG) alert, a tool available in many vendor EHRs and other clinical information systems. Individuals considered to be at high risk of being targets of snooping can have a BTG alert placed on their chart. This alert fires when someone tries to access the chart. Typically, a BTG alert will request the user to declare the reason they are entering the chart and require reentry of their password. Crucially, there is also the ability to back off via a "Cancel" button, thereby allowing self-deterrence at the brink of snooping. High rates of false positive firings of BTG alerts can generate alert fatigue, leading to disregard of alerts, so they should be used judiciously. Also, BTG alerts should not be used without a SAR program as BTG alerts may foster snooping, by giving a "green light," whenever an alert does not fire.

Why not use access controls to limit which patient records users can enter? First, because access restrictions do not deter snooping, they only limit its scope. More importantly, access restrictions, no matter how well thought out, can impede care and harm patients. Patients move around—from clinic or home to and from hospital, within and between hospitals. Transitions are a time of heightened risk of harm. Preventing receiving clinicians from accessing these patients' records greatly increases that risk. Clinicians also move around, covering for one another, often on short notice, working on different units or facilities on different days, and in some cases having multiple roles in the same organization. Finally, only the main responsibilities of a particular role can be perceived "at a distance" by those endeavoring to create access restrictions; equally important marginal and occasional responsibilities can be blocked. The patients most disadvantaged by access controls are those who are deteriorating quickly—and need clinicians, new to their care, to save their lives; and those considered high privacy risks. Therefore, unfortunately, access controls systematically threaten sick VIPs.

Just as development of an effective SAR and BTG program requires active collaboration with compliance, HR and line management leaders' development of approaches to protect against cyber threats, without impeding patient care, requires collaboration with security and other IT leaders. CISOs are charged with protecting the organization from ever-evolving attacks from myriad, often well-financed and sophisticated threat actors. They have difficult jobs—when things go well no one notices, but when a successful attack occurs, or their controls harm patients, they get blamed. By collaborating with a CMIO, a CISO can avoid initiatives that interfere with care and get help with implementing alternative balanced controls quickly and effectively.

The key to achieving optimal, balanced cyber and care delivery risk reduction is an effective security governance structure, which should include the most senior operational, clinical, compliance, and IT leaders as sponsors. At the highest level, this body formulates strategy and provides answers to the tough tradeoffs that must be made. A midlevel committee is also needed to assess options and produce recommendations to sponsors. Task-specific subcommittees and workgroups with IT, security, and clinical experts can develop and operationalize implementation plans. Such a governance approach allows an organization to effectively address questions such as: which websites, domains, or countries to block; when to use soft blocks (akin to BTG alerts) and when to use hard blocks (to prevent access). In addition, they can decide which roles have "elevated" privileges to databases and systems warranting special controls to prevent external access to those systems—and what those controls should consist of: password length, complexity, and expiry policies; when and how to require multifactor authentication (MFA); what and how to restrict mobile device functions and access; and many other questions.

In addition to a security governance structure, organizations should create written Major Breach plans, detailing who participates in what sorts of decisions, and whose decisions are final. Once documented, Major Breach exercises should be conducted periodically to exercise and test the plans, which should be continually modified based on learning. A healthcare organization that finds itself disabled by an attack will respond far more quickly and effectively if it already has a tested response plan in place.

CMIOs are critical players in security governance and decision-making, since they—often uniquely—understand the needs and perspectives of clinical care and of technology, and because they have knowledge and experience of how clinicians interact with information systems. CMIOs understand that technologic complexity should be managed by IT experts and hidden from clinicians so that they can focus on their patients. Similarly, CMIOs understand that the best way to drive a desired action is to make it the easiest path.

These learnings and approaches apply equally to privacy and security. MFA is an example. Requiring clinicians to enter their password and then also a one-time passcode (OTP) to log into an EHR would impose an enormous burden. Letting them associate their ID badge with their password when they first log in, and then let them tap their badge to log in for a defined number of hours without having to reenter their password is a gift, as is having the OTP be silently sent to the workstation from the clinician's phone via Bluetooth; all are MFA.

Deference to evidence is another powerful CMIO trait. Many organizations continue to routinely expire passwords, without any evidence to support the practice, ignoring white papers from Gartner and others demonstrating that this practice degrades security by forcing users to write down their passwords. Now that the National Institute of Standards and Technology (NIST) (2017) warns against routine expiry, this harmful practice will, hopefully, disappear.

CMIOs should consider privacy and security as core to their responsibilities as workflow, design, and clinical decision support. Privacy and security threats—and their organization's response to such threats—risk impeding or even destroying the work they have accomplished to support care delivery. Those CMIOs who have not done so, should wade into this space, by reaching out to their privacy, compliance, and security leaders and working with them to create the effective decision-making and rapid-response structures and processes that are needed. In so doing, CMIOs will build the relationships they will need to drive toward balanced decisions to reduce all risk—including that to patient safety and care quality. Ultimately, in the midst of a major breach, their voice will be heard.

References

National Institute of Standards and Technology. 2017. https://pages. nist.gov/800-63-3/sp800-63b.html. Accessed September 2017.
Silvester N. 2010. https://www.dailyrecord.co.uk/news/health/ doctor-who-hacked-into-prime-ministers-1047281. Accessed September 2017.

Chapter 13

The Role of the CMIO in Small Healthcare Organizations

Ronald W. Louks

Contents

Background

The importance of physician leadership in the healthcare system in general, including clinical informatics, cannot be overestimated...indeed this is the very premise for a book pertaining specifically to physician leadership in the HIT realm. While the need for established physician informatics leadership is widely accepted as a given by the C-suite and clinicians alike in academic and larger healthcare systems, this perception has been slower to filter downward into the HIT endeavors of smaller rural and community healthcare systems. Thus, the feeling that the EHR implementation was done to the physicians rather than by the physicians is even more prevalent in small healthcare organizations. And there is no question that in the rush to "cash in" on the incentive dollars (from programs that are addressed elsewhere in this book) earlier in this decade, many small healthcare organizations (as well as some larger ones) hastily implemented EHR physician applications with insufficient input from physicians and often inadequate preparation and training prior to go-live. Fortunately, most of the so-affected healthcare systems have since undertaken steps to engage their physicians and optimize their EHR technology in partnership with their medical staffs.

While many Critical Access Hospitals (CAHs) have added the CIO to their governance structure, far fewer have taken the additional step of incorporating the CMIO position, as such. However, the CMIO position is increasingly common in the systems a little bit above the CAH size. At many smaller healthcare organizations (especially CAHs) this role is often known simply as the "Physician Champion." Unfortunately, some small organizations saw the need for this role when they were first going live with their EHR, but then phased it out when they were "done." Every healthcare system needs ongoing physician informatics leadership regardless of the size of the organization, a fact that most small organizations now recognize. The EHR is a journey, not a destination...

The Job

The CMIO (or equivalent) in a small healthcare system will typically be a part-time physician informaticist and have most of their time devoted to clinical work. However, that ratio depends on the structure of the organization, overall size, number of clinics, specialties, ED volume, etc. This position may be filled by a physician already in the organization that steps up when the need for physician HIT leadership is identified. Having the respect of their peers is essential. A physician who has EHR experience prior to coming to the current facility and is still building his or her practice is often an ideal candidate, since they will be more likely to have some time to carve out of their schedule. Dedicated EHR admin time is a must, ideally no less than 20 percent of total compensation, commensurate with time spent performing this part of their duties. He or she must be willing to be an agent of change, and should anticipate that this may not sit well with some of their peers. And having what I like to call a "high tolerance for ambiguity" will also be an asset. The physician who steps up from within the ranks of the organization is unlikely to have had any formal informatics or leadership education and will definitely benefit from both. CMIO education is covered in another chapter of this book and is strongly encouraged...if not essential. Perusal of the CMIO job boards reveals that small organizations, even CAHs, are increasingly posting jobs for CMIOs. So, the part-time physician informaticist is definitely in demand and has a growing number of options for relocation if they prefer the smaller rural and community type of practice, as opposed to an urban setting.

The Challenge

It has been said that Ginger Rogers had to do everything that Fred Astaire did, but backwards and in heels. That is often how it feels to the physician informaticist (and everyone else, for that matter) in the small healthcare system. You are supposed to accomplish the same outcomes as the major urban centers but with fewer resources at your disposal while typically getting paid significantly less for your accomplishment. Most small organizations, especially those in rural areas, have great difficulty recruiting and retaining physicians. Consequently, 77 percent of the nation's 2041 rural counties are health professional shortage areas. According to the National Rural Health Association (2017), 20 percent of the U.S. population (which is older and sicker) lives in rural underserved areas but only 10 percent of physicians practice in these same areas. More than 40 percent of rural patients must travel 20-plus miles to receive specialty care, compared to 3 percent of metropolitan patients. 79 rural hospitals have closed since 2010 and another 673 rural hospitals are considered vulnerable, due to perennially operating at a loss. In just the past few years, rural hospitals have received tens of millions of dollars in Medicare reductions (loss of rural hospital designations and payments, sequestration cuts, and ACA cuts) (National Rural Health Association, 2017). Internet access is often less than optimal which creates difficulty in implementing and supporting an EHR in outlying clinics. Because of the shortage of resources, many small rural facilities are unable to upgrade their aging IT infrastructure. These are just a few of the challenges faced by many small healthcare organizations.

The Leadership

The success of an EHR implementation obviously involves significant IT components, but full adoption and optimization is also dependent on other non-IT factors. The leadership engagement of the C-suite, usually the CEO, is of paramount importance to the EHR adoption process in the small organization. Most physicians in large healthcare systems have already progressed through all five Kubler-Ross stages of grieving over the loss of their paper charts, and are by now generally at the "acceptance" stage (with occasional regression to depression and/or anger). But in some small organizations, especially CAHs, it is still possible to find physicians that are steadfastly affixed in the initial stage of "denial." Since many of the medical staff are often voluntary rather than employed by the facility, the C-suite may struggle with "making them use the EHR." While this battle typically must no longer be fought in larger systems, think of the potential impact on a small facility when a single physician that is resistant to using the EHR is responsible for 25 percent (or more) of hospital admissions and threatens to send patients to another facility. And, if this is a physician who has lived in the community for decades, they may know many of the hospital board members far better than the CEO does, or may in fact be a board member themselves. Politically charged situations such as this are not unusual in rural communities and puts the C-suite in a nearly untenable position. The CMIO at a small organization needs to have the full backing of the C-suite to be successful—something that CMIOs in larger organizations take for granted. If the C-suite allows certain physicians to bypass EHR usage, whether in whole or in part, this will create multiple divergent and dysfunctional workflows, much to the detriment of the organization and the chagrin of the CMIO. This is how some small resource strapped facilities that can least afford to support multiple dysfunctional workflows, unfortunately wind up doing just that. Most small organizations do quite well with physician adoption by exercising leadership, good communication, full transparency, and tireless physician engagement. Identifying the best workflow and process, then investing time with physicians and providing the proper training is essential to success.

The Team

Due to the widespread adoption of EHRs in response to the incentive programs of the past few years, it is increasingly unlikely that a system of any size would now be implementing their first EHR. However, EHR optimization should be an ongoing and continuous effort and is often necessitated by major upgrades and enhancements provided by EHR vendors. Since the CMIO (or equivalent) in the small healthcare organization may be spread a little thin and have a significant clinical workload, this makes the team around them that much more important. The importance of the EHR Committee and Clinical IT personnel cannot be overstated. Many small organizations formed an EHR Committee when they first went live with their EHR, but then made the mistake of disbanding this committee when they felt that they had achieved an acceptable level of EHR adoption. This is understandable, since in many small organizations key people often "wear multiple hats" and want to minimize unnecessary meetings. Some CAHs have departments that only have one full-time employee which makes attending meetings a challenge. However, due to ever-changing payer mandates, government regulations, and EHR updates, the EHR Committee serves a very important ongoing role and is an essential asset to the CMIO in the small organization. When proposing a change in workflow or process, or prior to implementing an upgrade or new functionality, this committee is the best resource to discuss potential system-wide implications and then participate in testing the proposed change(s). This can avoid many potential unforeseen and undesirable consequences.

Good Clinical IT personnel, ideally RNs, are an asset in any size organization. However, in the small organization (especially CAHs) the value of a good, full time Clinical IT nurse seems disproportionately higher compared to larger organizations. For the CMIO in the small organization, the Clinical IT nurse will be able to provide at-the-elbow assistance to the staff physicians that a part-time physician informaticist simply cannot always provide. A good Clinical IT nurse will also be very cognizant of clinical workflow and process and often have invaluable insight on EHR customization and enhancements that can positively impact physician usage of the EHR. Another potential resource is the EHR vendor, they will very likely have numerous education tools that can be taken advantage of (often online), as well as connect the CMIO with a peer resource at the vendor that will be able to provide valuable insight into how other organizations of a similar size succeeded with their EHR optimization.

The Goal

Much of the wisdom contained in the other chapters of this book is clearly applicable and readily scalable to the small healthcare organization. However, insufficient resources and lack of redundancy are often major obstacles for the CMIO in a small organization and can significantly limit or delay what they can accomplish. This is when that "high tolerance for ambiguity" helps you remain focused on what you can accomplish; prioritization is key. Don't let perfect be the enemy of good!

Reference

National Rural Health Association. 2017. https://www.ruralhealthweb. org/advocate. Accessed August 2017.

Chapter 14

Government, Guidance and the CXIO

Michael J. McCoy and Jacob Reider

Government requirements can be both a boon and a bane to citizens in general and to the health care leader in particular. Some regulations are needed to keep bad actors from doing bad things; as much as we all would like to believe that everyone is honest and trustworthy and has your best interests at heart, the sad reality is that is not the case. Government, be it local, state or federal, has the responsibility to provide a framework that reflects the three levels of engagement: (a) laws, which define principles of behavior, (b) regulations, which provide detailed requirements, and (c) guidance, which offers recommended (but not required) activities/processes. Unfortunately, government engagement at any (or all) of these levels can (and will) occasionally cause adverse unintended consequences due to imprecise language or due to policy decisions that may not have considered all possible outcomes.

Hopefully, though, understanding the distinctions between guidance, regulations, laws, and their various life cycles can help the CMIO/CHIO in discussing pathways to success within the health care organization or other setting. Following the path of proposed legislation is something only political junkies could find enjoyable, but having some inkling of what might come out of the sausage-making is important to properly advise politicians of the impact, intended or unintended, of proposed legislation. Once a law has been signed, it is up to the appropriate agency to craft regulations or guidance that complies, as that agency's own lawyers assert, with the passed law.

The federal process requires a notice of proposed rulemaking (NPRM) that outlines intended regulations, requesting comments from the public and stakeholders that will be considered (though not necessarily acted on) for the Final Rule. Government employees are not allowed to make *any* public statements on the NPRM, with the theory being that explaining what one meant by a particular word, phrase or sentence would deter comments, or influence how it (the wording) should be interpreted. Items that are delineated in the original NPRM may be deleted from a final rule, but new items are not allowed to be added (unless the item is a logical outgrowth of something within the NPRM). It can take a long time from the passage of a law to writing the NPRM (6 to 60 months or more), and similarly a long time to collate and respond to the comments on an NPRM for creation of a final rule (at least 6 months). The rule is reviewed by the agency/ division legal team, and then goes into "clearance," where the broader agency (and its divisions), other agencies impacted by the rule, and the executive branch all get to provide input into the final prose, and ideally ensure that their concerns are addressed. The intent is to provide transparency in the process, but of course the executive branch can, and does, influence or override other priorities.

Likewise, a change in administration can put the brakes on how existing regulations are implemented or enforced. Much as with speed limit signs, and knowing that it is illegal to exceed the posted limit, if the limit is thought to be too low, little enforcement may occur. If thought too high, aggressive enforcement could happen. Both of these could happen without a legislative change to the speed limit itself.

All of this is relevant in today's environment, though within bounds. It is important to note the distinction between *enforcing* an existing law (and the rules and regulations that arise from it) and *re-writing* a law. One cannot go back to a new congressional body and ask what something within a particular law means; only the original body would know that, and thus it falls to the internal lawyers (Office of the Inspector General, or OIG) for each agency to make that interpretation. Changing the law means new action by the legislative body. But an agency *can* change how it chooses to *enforce* parts of its own regulations, as long as the regulation still complies with the underlying law.

The laws, regulations and guidance that are probably of most interest to this readership are ones related to Health Insurance Portability and Accountability Act (HIPAA), the EHR Incentive Programs (Meaningful Use), MIPS, MACRA, and ONC Certification of health information technology. Helping leadership understand the why and the how of complying with HIPAA and with consumer engagement sections of current laws can be challenging, especially as some of the rules related to payment for meaningful use, MIPS and MACRA, all originating from the Centers for Medicare and Medicaid Services (CMS), are still in a state of flux with feedback being incorporated into the implementation of those rules (see above!).

With true bi-partisan support, legislation that passed and became Meaningful Use, supplanted subsequently by MIPS and MACRA, was aimed at improving health care delivery *and* containing costs. Thus, even with changes in some elements of the enforcement of various later stage meaningful use requirements, the long game is for more accountability in care delivery, and better outcomes for patients from that care, with payment reforms a requisite part of that equation. Your ability to articulate that will help position your institution for the inevitable coming changes.

Helping hospitals and physicians plan for the complexities of current and future federal or state regulations requires that the CMIO have familiarity with the intricate details of these regulations, and there are many misinterpretations of the regulations.

HIPAA is a prime example of a law that is often misinterpreted, with far too many people in health care using it as a shield to avoid sharing information rather than the positive guide it is intended to be. The Department of Health and Human Services (HHS) houses the Office of Civil Rights (OCR), which is responsible for HIPAA education and enforcement. OCR has a good library of materials that should help a CMIO build a sound knowledge foundation, and answer frequently asked questions: https://www.hhs.gov/hipaa/for-professionals/privacy/guidance/index.html.

While having an advanced degree in mathematics would seem to serve well in understanding the new CMS payment rules, being able to explain the pathway to the future is very important, particularly given the changing nature of many of those transitional rules. Part of that explanatory legwork is for the executive team, but a large part will also be for the physicians in private practice, as most won't be spending the time to understand the intricacies (or the possible impact on their revenues that these will have). This also represents an opportunity to engage with the technology developers to ensure that they are fully cognizant of the coming changes (they most likely are, and have a significant government relations staff to stay abreast *and* try to influence direction). Not all technology developers are on top of things, though, so it is incumbent on CMIOs to stay in that loop, too.

One part of the new requirements is for enhanced consumer engagement, including through Application Programming Interfaces (APIs) permitting individuals to connect applications (smartphone or otherwise) to care delivery organization health IT infrastructure. The technology required for that engagement is part of ONC's 2015

Standards and Certification regulations, but like many other requirements, having the software capability doesn't mean that an organization has actually turned it on. In order to truly benefit from these capabilities, continued cultural shifts are going to be required of clinicians and hospital leadership. While the number of patients going to portals or using APIs is currently low, perhaps it is because there is not yet sufficient value in visiting when all laboratory results are not available, or bi-directional communications are not enabled. Getting a message on the patient portal that one will receive a message back "within 5 business days" is hardly the kind of message that would encourage the continued use of that modality!

Helping to shape future laws and regulations is an area in which organized medicine, physicians and hospitals can be (and have been) particularly effective. Specialty societies and trade associations for hospitals and other providers along the continuum of care lobby elected officials and civil servants to help convey points of view that might be missed or ignored. Active participation as a CMIO in your own specialty society is important, as is participation in other forums where voices combined can be effective in communicating issues and concerns to congressional staff and to executive branch agencies, particularly during NPRM comment periods before the final rules are issued.

While there are a few physicians that have been elected to high offices, for the most part, congressional staffers are the people that actually become deeply knowledgeable on a subject (such as health care technology), and educating them on the issues is critical. Interestingly, civil servants are not allowed to brief congressional staffers unless they are specifically invited to do so by the staffers! Industry or specialty societies don't have the same limitations interacting with congressional staff. And, as we have seen with the latest administration and Congress, passing legislation is hard, particularly when a common vision is lacking. Influencing rulemaking through the Federal Register process can be very effective (or a good backstop) for achieving balanced and reasonable regulation.

Working for a government agency is an interesting option for some people. It is an amazing place to work with dedicated and passionate people trying to make a difference in the world. The top people leading each agency are appointed to their jobs by the executive branch (White House, Governor, etc.). Depending on the size of that agency, department or division, that may equate to one or more political appointees, often referred to as "politicals."

The civil servants who are the mainstay of day-to-day operations are, to a large degree, protected from the administrative changes that occur with each election cycle. The agency or division will have staff, including those with legal backgrounds, dedicated to the rulemaking process. Much as in the developer world where individuals writing code for the electronic technology system aren't actually clinicians, and thus don't fully understand the "thoughtflow" of clinicians, those writing regulations for implementing laws often have only a few clinical people advising them. The challenges of working in a government agency relate to helping bring a balance of real-world perspective versus the legal requirements of writing rules and regulations (again, see above!). It is still very interesting to hear the varied perspectives on why a particular item should or should not be included in a rule, recognizing that usually *someone* has requested a particular item. When I worked at ONC, I was once in a meeting with leaders from a number of specialty societies. Everyone attending was decrying the number of requirements in ONC's certification of EHRs. Yet one person said out loud, "But, *we* (Specialty 'P') need *more* requirements in the Certification Regulations to *make* the vendors do X."

The clinical people that I worked with were just as dedicated to ensuring the work being done was relevant, accurate, and positively impactful as anyone directly caring for patients. Perhaps to a larger degree, attention was paid to the public health and "greater good" aspects of the care delivery system, recognizing the spend that has occurred and the value-based care paradigm that is being promoted.

There are many government agencies wherein the interests of informaticians would fit well, from local to federal. Informaticists understand that the that the overlap of population health, informatics, genomics, and precision medicine have great potential to improve the quality and longevity of people's lives. This knowledge is critical to guiding these agencies in their support of health information technology. At the federal level, there are many agencies that could be of interest (e.g., HHS [which includes the FDA, Center for Disease Control (CDC), CMS, Indian Health Services, and ONC], the VA and the Social Security Administration). The pay is not particularly high, so those working for the government are doing so out of a sense of duty and a desire to help do good things. It is a great educational opportunity to see and experience this segment of our society, especially given the enormous impact the actions of the government can have on health care and the work done providing it. Do be mindful that, in this space, immediate gratification is unlikely, and thus setting realistic goals and expectations is essential to workplace happiness.

I consider it an honor and privilege to have worked at ONC, and I left having made many lifelong friends. There are many really smart people working in that office, and their passion and dedication to the mission cannot be overstated. I have great admiration for those who continue working there to advance the support of technology in delivering better outcomes at a lower cost.

Index